New Zealand
North Island

Darroch Donald

New Canaan
Library
Connect · Discover · Grow

New Canaan Library
151 Main Street
New Canaan, CT 06840
www.newcanaanlibrary.org

Credits

919.31
F

Footprint credits

Editor: Jo Williams
Production and layout: Emma Bryers
Maps: Kevin Feeney

Managing Director: Andy Riddle
Commercial Director: Patrick Dawson
Publisher: Alan Murphy
Publishing Managers: Felicity Laughton,
Jo Williams, Nicola Gibbs
Marketing and Partnerships Director:
Liz Harper
Marketing Executive: Liz Eyles
Trade Product Manager: Diane McEntee
Account Managers: Paul Bew, Tania Ross
Advertising: Renu Sibal, Elizabeth Taylor
Trade Product Co-ordinator: Kirsty Holmes

Photography credits

Front cover: Dreamstime
Back cover: Shutterstock

Printed in the United States of America

Publishing information

Footprint *Focus New Zealand North Island*
1st edition
© Footprint Handbooks Ltd
September 2012

ISBN: 978 1 908206 83 1
CIP DATA: A catalogue record for this book
is available from the British Library

® Footprint Handbooks and the Footprint
mark are a registered trademark of
Footprint Handbooks Ltd

Published by Footprint
6 Riverside Court
Lower Bristol Road
Bath BA2 3DZ, UK
T +44 (0)1225 469141
F +44 (0)1225 469461
footprinttravelguides.com

Distributed in the USA by Globe Pequot
Press, Guilford, Connecticut

Every effort has been made to ensure that
the facts in this guidebook are accurate.
However, travellers should still obtain advice
from consulates, airlines, etc, about travel
and visa requirements before travelling.
The authors and publishers cannot accept
responsibility for any loss, injury or
inconvenience however caused.

The content of Footprint *Focus New Zealand
North Island* has been taken directly from
Footprint's *New Zealand* which was
researched and written by Darroch Donald.

Contents

Brush aside the jet lag and any preconceptions surrounding New Zealand and the inevitable expectations of mountain ranges, and Auckland will prove to be a pleasant surprise. Here you can marvel at how a metropolis almost the size of LA can really be so beautiful.

Eager to head for the hills, most join the great Maui or Britz migrations south. But those with more time head north instead. It's a wise move. Northland is dubbed the cradle of the nation and up there you will experience some of the best examples of Maoridom and get a true taste of just how beautiful New Zealand is. Head south and it is rude not to go via the Coromandel. In the holiday season it is considered Auckland's principal stress buster. Here, beautiful coastal scenery gels with that laid-back atmosphere for which the country is famous.

The TVZ, or Taupo Volcanic Zone, is one of the most active in the world and has been shaping the history of Central North Island for thousands of years. Perhaps the region's most obvious feature is Lake Taupo (the country's largest), home to a bustling tourist town and renowned for its world-class trout fishing and adventure activities. Steeped in Maori legend, Tongariro National Park boasts the active volcanoes of Ngauruhoe and Ruapehu, excellent skiing and walking. With its rich Maori heritage Rotorua has served as one of the country's major tourist destinations for years.

East of Wellington, gateway to the South Island, the rash of wineries around Martinborough and the scenic drive to Cape Palliser are just two of the great attractions of the Wairarapa Region, while Kapiti Island to the north offers a fascinating insight in to the country's unique and once prolific birdlife.

Planning your trip

Getting to New Zealand

Being an island nation and 'last stop from anywhere', the majority of international visitor arrive by air and in to Auckland New Zealand's largest city and airport. Over recent year cruise ship visits have increased, but passengers are tied to a limited onshore itinerary.

Air

From Europe The main route is usually via Heathrow or Frankfurt, either west with a stopover in the USA (Los Angeles), or east with stopovers in Southeast Asia or the Middle East. The Australasian airline market is currently very volatile and prices vary. The cheapest return flights, off-season (May-August), will be around £800 (€931), rising to at least £1100 (€1281) around Christmas. Mainstream carriers include **Air New Zealand** ① *airnewzealand.com*, and **Qantas** ① *qantas.com* (west via the USA); and **Singapore Airlines** ① *singapore air.com*; **Thai Air** ① *thaiair.com*; **Air Malaysia** ① *malaysiaairlines. com*, and **Emirates** ① *emirates.com* (all east via Asia, or the Middle East). As usual the best bargains are to be found online.

From the Americas Competition is fierce with several operators including **Air New Zealand** ① *airnewzealand.com*; **Qantas** ① *qantas.com*; **Air Canada** ① *aircanada.com* and **Lufthansa** ① *lufthansa.com*, all offering flights from Los Angeles (LAX) or San Francisco (SFO) to Auckland. One of the cheapest is the new Richard Branson venture **VAustralia** ① *vaustralia.com.au*, that offers good deals via Sydney. **Air Canada** ① *aircanada.com*, and **United** ① *united.com*, connecting with Alliance partners at LAX fly from Vancouver, Toronto and Montreal. Prices range from CAN$1650-2700. There are also direct flights from Buenos Aires to Auckland with **Aerolíneas Argentinas**, *aerolineas.com.ar*, flying out of New York and Miami.

The cost of a standard return in the low season (May-August) from LAX starts from around US$1050, from New York from US$1500 and Chicago from US$1450. In the high season add about US$300 to the standard fare.

The flight time between LAX and Auckland is around 12½ hours.

From Australia As you might expect there is a huge choice and much competition with trans-Tasman flights, in fact it is corporate warfare. Traditionally most flights used to go from Cairns, Brisbane, Sydney and Melbourne to Auckland but now many of the cheaper flights can actually be secured to Wellington, Christchurch, Dunedin and Queenstown.

Flights and especially ski package deals to Queenstown can also be cheaper and have been heavily promoted in recent years, but conditions usually apply, giving you limited flexibility. At any given time there are usually special deals on offer from the major players like **Qantas** ① *qantas.com.au*; Qantas subsidiary **JetStar** ① *jetstar.com.au*; **Air New Zealand** ① *airnewzealand.com.au*, and **Pacific Blue** ① *pacificblue.com.au*, so again shop around and online. Prices range from AUS$270-750 return. The flight time between Sydney and Auckland is three hours, Melbourne three hours 45 minutes.

Don't miss...

Airport information The two principal international airports in New Zealand are **Auckland** ① *T0800 247767, auckland-airport.co.nz*, in the North Island and **Christchurch** ① *T64 3353 7774, christchurch-airport.co.nz*, in the South. Auckland is by far the most utilized and better served of the two with direct flights worldwide, while Christchurch deals mainly with connecting flights via or to Australia. Additionally, Wellington, Dunedin and Queenstown also serve the East Coast of Australia.

Auckland airport is 21 km south of the city centre. **Shuttle bus** ① *airbus.co.nz*, or taxis are the main transport services to the city and they depart regularly from outside the terminal building. The airbus will cost about $15 one-way $22 return, a taxi around $60. There is no rail link.

Transport in New Zealand

Public transport in all its forms (except rail) is generally both good and efficient. All the main cities and provincial towns can be reached easily by air or by road. Although standard fares can be expensive there are a vast number of discount passes and special seasonal deals available, aimed particularly at the young independent traveller. Although it is entirely possible to negotiate the country by public transport, for sheer convenience you are advised to get your own set of wheels. Fuel prices compare favourably to most of Europe ($2.20 for unleaded, $1.50 for diesel).

Air
Domestic air travel If you do not have your own hired or private vehicle then at least a few domestic flights are worth considering, especially between the islands. Currently **Air New Zealand** ① *T0800-737000, airnewzealand.co.nz*; Qantas subsidiary **Jetstar** ① *T0800-800995, jetstar.com*; and **Pacific Blue** ① *T0800-670000, pacificblue.co.nz*, are the principal air carriers providing services between Auckland, Christchurch and Wellington and most regional centres. A one-way ticket from Auckland to Christchurch can be bought online for as little as $50.

Road
Bus National bus travel in New Zealand is well organized and the networks and daily schedules are good. Numerous shuttle companies service the South Island and there are also many local operators and independent companies that provide shuttles to accommodation establishments, attractions and activities. These are listed in the Transport sections of the main travelling text.

The main bus companies are **Intercity** ① *intercitycoach.co.nz*, and **Newmans** ① *newmanscoach.co.nz*. They often operate in partnership. For information and reservations call the following regional centres: Auckland T09-583 5780; Wellington T04-385 0520 and Christchurch T03-365 1113. Intercity operates in both the North and South Islands, while Newmans operate throughout the North Island, except in Northland where **Northliner Express** ① *T09-307 5873, northliner.co.nz*, co-operates with Intercity. Also popular are **Nakedbus.com**, which uses the same model of low overheads and internet-only booking service that the cheap airlines do. It has managed to undercut long-established companies

All the major companies offer age, student and backpacker concessions as well as a wide variety of flexible national or regional travel passes with some in combination with the interisland ferry and rail.

Car Other than a campervan this is by far the best way to see New Zealand. Most major international hire companies and many national companies are in evidence. You may also consider buying a vehicle for the trip and selling it again afterwards but research prices thoroughly and get the vehicle independently checked by the AA (aa.co.nz). There are specialist markets in both Auckland and Christchurch (backpackerscarmarket.co.nz).

A hire vehicle will give you the flexibility and freedom needed to reach the more remote and beautiful places. Outside the cities traffic congestion and parking is rarely a problem. In New Zealand you drive on the left (though most Aucklanders drive where they like). Make sure you familiarize yourself with the rules before setting out (NZ Road Code booklets are available from AA offices). The speed limit on the open road is 100 kph and in built-up areas it is 50 kph. Police patrol cars and speed cameras are omnipresent so if you speed you will almost certainly be caught. A valid driving license from your own country or an international license is required and certainly must be produced if you rent a vehicle. Parking in the cities can be very expensive. Do not risk parking in restricted areas or exceeding your time allotment on meters. Finally, never leave or hide valuables in your car and lock it at all times.

If you are travelling in a bought second-hand vehicle you are advised to join **The New Zealand Automobile Association (AA)** ① *T09-966 8800, T0800-500555, aa.co.nz; breakdowns, T0800-500222*. It also provides a great range of maps and travelling information as well as the usual member benefits. The annual membership fee of around $80 will provide basic breakdown assistance.

Good private deals can be secured with second-hand vehicles through trademe.co.nz but always get a car checked mechanically by an independent entity and do a police check for previous fines, etc (aa.co.nz).

Motor homes New Zealand is well geared up for campervan hire and travel and there's an accompanying glut of reputable international companies. Being a fairly compact country it is certainly a viable way to explore with complete independence. Although hire costs may seem excessive, once you subtract the inevitable costs of accommodation, provided you are not alone and can share those costs, it can work out cheaper in the long run. You will find that motor camps are available even in the more remote places and a powered site will cost $20-30 per night for two people. Note that lay-by parking is illegal and best avoided. Again, like car rental rates, campervan rates vary and are seasonal. Costs are rated on a sliding scale according to model, season and length of hire. The average daily charge for a basic two-berth/six-berth for hire over 28 days, including insurance is $195/295 in the high season and $75/120 in the low season. The average campervan works out at about

4-16 litres per 100 km in petrol costs. Diesel is cheaper than petrol but at present more harmful to the environment.

The most popular rental firms are **Jucy** ① *T0800-399736, T09-374 4360, jucy.co.nz*; **Maui/Britz** ① *T0800-651080, T00-800-20080801, maui.co.nz, britz.co.nz*; **Kea Campers** ① *T0800-520052, T09-4417833, keacampers.com*, and for more unconventional vehicles, **Spaceships** ① *T0800-SPACE SHIPS, T09-5262130, spaceships.tv*, which offers Toyota People Movers or campervan hybrids complete with DVD and double bed.

Ferry

Other than a few small harbour-crossing vehicle ferries and the short trip to Stewart Island from Bluff in Southland, the main focus of ferry travel is of course the inter-island services across Cook Strait. The two ports are Wellington at the southern tip of the North Island and Picton in the beautiful Marlborough Sounds on the South Island.

There are two services: the **Interislander** ① *T0800-802802, T04-4983302, interislander.co.nz*, and the smaller of the two companies **Bluebridge** ① *T0800-844844, T04-4716188, bluebridgeco.nz*.

A standard vehicle with two passengers will cost about $265 one-way, a motor home with two passengers $365 and two passengers no vehicle $53 per person.

Train

For years the rail network in New Zealand has struggled to maintain anything other than a core network between its main population centres. However, that said, the trains in themselves are pretty comfortable, the service is good and the stunning scenery will soon take your mind off things. Within the North Island there is a daily service (Friday, Saturday and Sunday in winter) between Auckland and Wellington known as the Overlander. Within the South Island, the daily services between Picton and Christchurch (the TranzCoastal and Christchurch to Greymouth (the TranzAlpine) are both world-class journeys. For detail contact **TranzScenic** ① *T0800-872467, T04-4950775, tranzscenic.co.nz*.

Also, designed specifically as a tourist attraction, the **Taieri Gorge Railway** ① *T03-477 4449, taieri.co.nz*, runs from Dunedin to Middlemarch and back, with shuttle connections to Queenstown.

All fares are of a single class, but prices range greatly from 'standard' to 'super saver' so check carefully what you are entitled to and what deals you can secure.

Where to stay in New Zealand

New Zealand offers the full range of tourist accommodation from exclusive luxury lodges to basic campsites. Indeed, such is the sheer variety that the only limitation beyond the budget is your own imagination.

Given the compact nature of the country, its modern infrastructure and in no small part its awesome natural aesthetics, many choose the independent option and hire a motor home or a campervan, or if on a limited budget purchase a vehicle temporarily for the trip. Then, by staying predominantly at motor parks, flexibility and freedom can be maximised. This is by far the best and most popular option in New Zealand and the kiwi tourism industry is well geared up for it.

But whatever accommodation you choose you will find a huge range on offer with the local and regional visitor information centres (i-SITES) or internet being the best places to both source and to book. There are also many books available including the

Price codes

Where to stay

$$$$	more than $200 per night
$$	$50-100

$$$ $100-200
$ under $50

Price is for a double room in high season.

Restaurants

$$$ more than $30 $$ $20-30 $ under $20

Price is per person for a 2-course meal with a drink, including service and cover charge.

AA accommodation guides (aaguides.co.nz) as well as numerous motor parks, motels campsites and backpacker guides.

In the high season (November to March) and particularly around Christmas and the first two weeks in January you are advised to book all types of accommodation at least three days in advance.

Hotels

Hotels in New Zealand can generally be listed under one of four categories: large luxury hotels; chain hotels; boutique hotels; and budget hotels.

There are plenty of luxurious (four- to five-star) hotels in the major cities and prices range from $250-1000 per night. As you would expect, all rooms are equipped with the latest technology. They also have restaurants and leisure facilities including swimming pools, spa pools and gyms.

Standard chain hotels are commonplace, vary in both age and quality and include names such as Quality Hotels, Novotel and Copthorne. Found in all major cities and the larger provincial towns, their standard prices range from $130-300 but they have regular weekend or off-season deals. Most have restaurants, pools and a gym.

Boutique hotels vary in size and price but tend to be modern and of a luxurious standard. The smaller, more intimate boutique hotels are overtaking the major chains in popularity. On average double rooms here can cost anything from $175-400.

Given the flourishing backpacker industry in New Zealand, budget hotels struggle to exist and most often you will find the generic title equates to exactly that.

Lodges and B&Bs

There are a growing number of luxury lodges throughout the country and most sell themselves on their location as much as their architecture, sumptuous rooms, facilities and cuisine. Prices tend to be high, ranging from $200 to a mind-bending $2600 per night (which equates to almost eight months in a well-equipped motor park). B&Bs are not as common in New Zealand as they are in Europe, but can still be found in most places. They vary greatly in style, size and quality and can be anything from a basic double room with shared bathroom and a couple of boiled eggs for breakfast to a luxurious ensuite or self-contained unit with the full cooked breakfast. Again prices vary, with the standard cost being as little as $75-100. Many lodges and B&Bs also offer evening meals. Again, the visitor information centres (i-SITES) are the best place to both source and book.

Home and farmstays

Generally speaking if an establishment advertises itself as a homestay it will deliberately lack the privacy of the standard B&B and you are encouraged to mix with your hosts. The idea is that you get an insight into Kiwi life, but it may or may not be for you depending on your preferences and personality.

Farmstays of course give you the added agricultural and rural edge, and are generally recommended. Accommodation can take many forms from being in-house with your hosts or fully self-contained, and breakfasts and evening meals are often optional. You may find yourself helping to round up sheep or milking a cow and if you have kids (farmstays usually welcome them) they will be wonderfully occupied for hours.

Both homestays and farmstays tend to charge the same, or slightly lower, rates as B&Bs. **New Zealand Farm Holidays** ① *T09-412 9649, nzfarmholidays.co.nz*, based near Auckland, produces a helpful free catalogue listing about 300 establishments.

Motels

Motels are still the preferred option of the average Kiwi holidaymaker and business traveller. They are everywhere and reproducing furtively. They vary greatly, from the awful, stained 1950s love shacks to the new and luxurious condos with bubbly spa pool. There is usually a range of rooms available and almost all have at least a shower, kitchen facilities and a TV – though whether it actually works and has Sky TV (or doubles as a plant pot) depends on the price. Most are clean, comfortable and well appointed, while in others you may find yourself trying to sleep next to the main road. Prices vary from studio units at about $75-85, one-bedroom units from $85-120 and suites accommodating families and groups for an additional charge for each adult. Many of the bigger and better establishments have a restaurant and a swimming pool. Many also make the most of the country's thermal features and have spas, sometimes even in your room.

Hostels

New Zealand is well served with hostels and budget accommodation establishments. Naturally, they vary greatly in age, design, location and quality. Some enjoy a busy atmosphere in the centre of town while others provide a quiet haven in the country. They also have a range of types of bedrooms on offer, with many having separate double and single rooms as well as the traditional dormitory. Dorms are usually single sex but sometimes optionally mixed. Camping facilities within the grounds are also common. Generally, hostels are good places to meet other travellers, managers are usually very knowledgeable and helpful; pick-ups are often free. Bikes, kayaks or other activity gear can often be hired at low cost or are free to use. Wherever you stay you will have access to equipped kitchens, a laundry, games or TV room, plenty of local information and, of course, phones and the internet. Prices vary little for a dorm bed, from $20 depending on season. Single rooms and doubles tend to be around $55, or about $30 per adult. In the high season and especially over Christmas through to March you are advised to pre-book everywhere at least three days in advance.

There are several major backpacking membership organizations in New Zealand that provide hostel listings and discounts.

Budget Backpacker Hostels Ltd (BBH) ① *T03-379 3014, bbh.co.nz*, has around 350 member establishments that must meet certain minimum quality criteria. These are listed in its Blue Book (free from i-SITES) along with handy descriptions, contact details and location maps of each hostel.

Qualmark…

The Qualmark star grading system, which is the official tourist operator star grading system in New Zealand, can help you choose the type of accommodation you are looking for, in the style that suits you.

It ranges from 1 star (Acceptable), through 5 stars (Exceptional), with an additional category 'Exclusive' (Outstanding). Look out for the black and yellow signs with silver fern logo.

The **YHA (Youth Hostel Association NZ)** ① *T0800-278299/T03-379 9970, yha.co.nz,* is part of a worldwide organization and they have about 70 establishments throughout New Zealand; the vast majority are associates as opposed to YHA owned and operated. Being part of a large organization, most are on a par if not better than the independent backpacker hostels. They all offer very much the same in standard of accommodation and facilities. They are also to be congratulated on their intensive eco-friendly policies with recycling not only provided in most hostels, but actively and enthusiastically embraced.

YHAs are only open to members but you can join in your home country (if YHA exists) or in New Zealand for an annual fee of $40 ($30 for renewals). Non-members can also stay at hostels for an additional charge of $3 per night. YHA membership cards can also entitle you to a number of discounts, including up to 30% off air and bus travel. Pick up the YHA Accommodation and Hostel Guide at any major i-SITE visitor centre.

Motor parks camps and cabins

New Zealand's fairly compact size and quality road network lends itself to road touring and it is very well served with quality motor parks and campsites. In fact, it is hailed as one of the best in the world. Motor parks can be found almost everywhere and not necessarily just in towns. The quality and age does of course vary. Some are modern and well equipped while others are basic. Almost all motor parks have laundry facilities and a few will charge a small fee ($0.20-1) for hot showers. Prices are generally very reasonable and range from $10-15 per person (child half price) for non-powered sites. Powered sites are often the same price or a few dollars more.

Most motor parks have a range of cabins from dog kennels to well-appointed alpine-type huts. They vary in price starting with a standard cabin with little more than a bed and electric socket for a mere $35 to a cabin with better facilities for up to $60 per night (for two) with an additional charge of $12-15 per person after that.

The **Top Ten** chain of motor parks, which has almost 50 nationwide, though up to $3 more expensive per night, is generally highly recommended (top10.co.nz).

Wild camping

'Where can I camp?' 'Assume nothing – always ask a local' is the catch-cry of the authorities and rightly so – wild camping with no respect for property and environment is not tolerated. The best advice is to stick to designated sites and to source them ask at the local visitor information centre (i-SITE), or regional Department of Conservation (DoC) office (doc.govt.nz). The website camping.org.nz is also useful.

The DoC has more than 100 basic campsites all over the country with many being in prime locations. They tend to provide clean running water, toilet facilities and BBQ areas, but rarely allow open fires. The national parks in particular are all excellently facilitated with comfortable well-equipped huts. There is usually a nightly fee of $2-10. Fees for huts

re anything from $5-40 per night depending on category and location. If you plan to use
DoC campsites and huts you are advised to research their locations, fee structures, rules
and regulations and book well in advance.

Food and drink in New Zealand

Budget permitting, you are in for a treat. The quality of food in New Zealand is superb.
Although there are many types of traditional cuisine and restaurants in evidence, the
principal style is Pacific Rim. It dips into the culinary heritage of many of the cultures of the
Oceania region as well as further afield like Europe. For dishes that have a distinctly Kiwi
edge look out for the lamb (arguably the best in the world), pork, venison and freshwater
fish like salmon or trout – though note you cannot buy trout commercially.

As you might expect there is also a heavy emphasis on seafood. The choice is vast with
many warm-water fish like snapper of particular note. Other seafood delights include
crayfish (the South Pacific equivalent to the lobster), oysters, paua (abalone), scallops
and the famous green-lipped mussels. There are also some treats in store from below the
ground. The kumara (sweet potato) will shed a whole new light on the humble spud, while
many of the international vegetables like asparagus and broccoli come cheap (especially
while in season) and are always fresh. From the tree the fruit of choice is of course the
succulent kiwi fruit, which although not exclusively grown in New Zealand is deservedly
celebrated. A traditional dessert in New Zealand is the pavlova; a sort of mountainous cake
made of meringue and whipped cream. For a real traditional treat try a Maori *hangi* or
feast. Prepared properly and without ketchup you will be amazed at just how good and
different fish, meat and vegetables can taste when cooked underground.

Eating out

There are eateries to suit every taste and budget from the ubiquitous fast-food joints to
world-class seafood restaurants. Auckland and Wellington (the latter has more cafés and
restaurants per capita than New York) are particularly rich in choice with a vast selection
of cafés, café-bars, brasseries and specialist international restaurants giving added puff to
the celebrated Pacific Rim.

Eating out in New Zealand is generally good value, especially given the usually
favourable foreign exchange rates. The vast majority of eateries fall into the 'mid-range'
bracket ($18-25 for a main). Most cafés open for breakfast between 0700 and 0900 and
stay open until at least 1700, and often until late into the evening or the early hours. This
usually applies seven days a week with special Sunday brunch hours provided. Most mid-
range restaurants open their doors daily for lunch (often 1100-1400) and dinner (from
1800). The more exclusive establishments usually open for dinner from about 1800, with
some (especially in winter) only opening some weekday evenings and at weekend

Vegetarians are generally well catered for in the main centres and provincial towns.

Self-catering

If you intend to do your own cooking, supermarkets offer a wide choice of fare and are often
open until around 2200. The main chains include Big Fresh, Woolworths and New World,
with Pac-n-Save and Countdown being marginally cheaper. For fresh fruit and vegetables,
stick to the numerous roadside or wholesale fruit markets where the difference in price
and quality can be astonishing. If touring via motor parks always check to see if they have
camp kitchen facilities as standards vary.

Drinks

Other than 'L&P' (a fairly unremarkable soft drink hailing from Paeroa in the Waikato, North Island) New Zealand lacks a national drink. If there is one, it is the highly sub-standard and over-rated beer called Lion Red or branded bottled beers like 'Steinlager'. Rest assured however, that all the main internationally well-known bottled beers are available, as are some good foreign tap ales like Guinness.

Beer and lager is usually sold by the 'handle', the 'glass' (pint) or the 'jug' (up to three pints). Half-pints come in a 12-fl oz (350 ml) glass. Rarely is a pint a proper imperial pint it's usually just under. Drinks generally cost $7-8 for a pint, about $5-6 for a jug of cheaper domestic beers and up to $8 for a double shot of spirit. Alcohol is much cheaper in rural pubs and RSAs (Retired Servicemen's Associations), where you can usually get yourself signed in. The minimum drinking age has just been reduced from 21 to 18. Liquor shops (off licenses) are everywhere and alcohol can generally (in most places) be bought seven days a week. There is also a thriving coffee culture almost everywhere in the main towns and cities, so you will not go without your daily caffeine fix.

New Zealand's diversity of climates and soil types has borne an equally rich array of wines and after over a century of development the country now boasts many internationally recognized labels. Hawke's Bay and Nelson/Marlborough areas are the principal wine-producing regions. New Zealand Sauvignon Blanc is rated throughout the world as one of the best, but there is growing recognition for its Chardonnay, Pinot Noir, Cabernet Sauvignon and Merlot. The choice is vast and whether a connoisseur or a novice you are advised to experiment. If you can, visit one of the many vineyards that offer tastings and cellar sales. For more information about New Zealand wines refer to nzwine. com or winesnewzealand.co.nz.

Entertainment in New Zealand

Despite the diminishing and undeserved reputation as a cultural backwater, New Zealand's entertainment scene is fresh and exciting. The major centres all boast numerous contemporary and historical venues that vie for a host of first-class domestic and international concerts and shows. Theatre, orchestral concerts, ballet, dance, comedy, rock and jazz are all well represented and annual or biennial festivals often attract well-known international acts. On a smaller scale you will find a vibrant nightlife in New Zealand cities and major provincial towns. Although not necessarily world class, the nightclubs, cabarets, pubs and local rock concerts will certainly have you shaking your pants. There's even Country and Western and line dancing. New Zealand also boasts two large, modern, 24-hour casinos in Wellington. Ticketek are the national administrators for information and ticketing and a full listing of shows and events can be sourced from their website, ticketek. co.nz or nzlive.com. The local press and national newspapers also have comprehensive entertainment events listings particularly at weekends (nzherald.co.nz).

Pubs and bars

The pub scene has come on in leaps and bounds over the last decade with new establishments opening up almost everywhere and shaking off the basic tavern and hotel image. Before the 1990s the vast majority of pubs in New Zealand were the archetypal male bastions and the type of establishments where ashtrays were built into the tables, pictures of the local hairy rugby team adorned the walls and the average Saturday night consisted of a good argument about sport, a band playing Deep Purple's Smoke on the

Water, followed by a fight, copious wall-to-wall vomiting and a failed attempt to get home. Of course such places still exist in some rural outposts, but generally speaking, pubs and bars are now a much more refined and classy affair, yet still retain that congenial and laid-back traditional pub atmosphere. New Zealand has also caught on to the pseudo Irish pub fad and although some are gimmicky, others are very good, offering fine surroundings and beer to match. Many drinking establishments are also now attached to restaurants and cafés with outdoor seating. In December 2004 it became illegal to smoke in all pubs, restaurants and cafés in New Zealand, though many still provide segregated (legal) areas outside. Pubs and bars are generally open from 1100-2230 with many having an extended license to 2400 and sometimes even 0300 at weekends.

Clubs

The cities and major towns all have their fair share of nightclubs that consistently pump up the volume to whatever is the latest international vibe. Some, particularly in Auckland, often attract touring international DJs.

The central business district obviously contains the most venues and a good idea for sourcing the best is to ask the staff at the largest backpacker establishments, or the barmen and women of the classiest bars. There is often a cover charge and dress is smart casual.

Gay and lesbian

Like their trans-Tasman counterparts, New Zealand cities have a welcome and thriving gay scene and the nightclubs and bars particularly around K'Road and Ponsonby in Auckland are a focus for it. Of course this only adds to both the atmosphere and the fun.

Each February Auckland hosts the popular 'Hero Festival' – the national gay event of the year. The festival involves a street parade and entertainment in the Ponsonby area (hero. org.nz). Although certainly not on the scale of the world-famous Sydney Mardi Gras, it is enjoyed by thousands, both gay and straight. How could one, for example, possibly resist 'Drag Aerobics with Buffy and Bimbo' (buffyandbimbo.com)?

There are a number of specialist publications and independent groups to source the latest news, events and information, including gaypages.co.nz, pinkpagesnet.com/newzealand, gaynewzealand.com and gaytravelnet.com/nz.

Publications to look out for in the main centres include the long-established **Gay Express** (gayexpress.co.nz).

Music concerts and festivals

Many international rock stars now include at least one gig in Auckland in their itinerary, often as an adjunct to Australian gigs and they are easily accommodated in the outdoor sports stadiums or purpose-built facilities like Auckland's new Vector Arena.

The country also has its fair share of city- and region-based music festivals, including the Big Day Out (Auckland, January, bigdayout.com) and The World of Music and Dance Festival WOMAD (Taranaki, July, womad.co.nz).

Festivals in New Zealand

A huge range of events and festivals are held throughout the year, ranging from th bizarre World of Wearable Art Awards to the spectacular Opera in the Park in Auckland.

i-SITES have listings of events and the NZTB website, purenz.com, or nzlive.com, hav detailed nationwide events listings.

Feb

Waitangi Day (Waitangi and nationwide) The nation recognizes Waitangi Day, 6 Feb, with a public holiday and by staging various national or regional events to commemorate the signing of The Treaty of Waitangi, New Zealand's founding document in 1840.

Art Deco Weekend (Napier) artdeconapier. com. Napier gears up and dresses up for its biggest annual event celebrating its internationally recognized art deco heritage. Charleston anyone?

New Zealand International Festival of the Arts (Wellington) nzfestival.co.nz. Biennial multi-arts festival held in the capital city and considered the nation's premier cultural event (next in 2014).

Pasifika Festival (Auckland) aucklandcity. govt.nz. A colourful, 1-day celebration of all of this Pacific Island, with contemporary arts and music, traditional food, crafts and cultural performances.

Apr

National Jazz Festival (Tauranga) jazz.org. nz. Founded in 1962 and held every Easter, this is oldest and the largest celebration of jazz in the country.

May

New Zealand International Comedy Festiva comedyfestival.co.nz. Held simultaneously over 3 weeks in Auckland and Wellington and featuring well-known and emerging domestic and international talent.

Sep

World of Wearable Art Awards (Wellington) worldofwearableart.com. First begun in 1987 in New Zealand's arts capital Nelson, this has grown to become one of New Zealand's most unusual and successful events, described as 'Mardis Gras meets Haute Couture'.

Essentials A-Z

Children

Families and travellers with children will generally find New Zealand very child friendly and replete with all the usual concessions for travel and activities. With so many outdoor activities safety is a natural concern, but this is nothing common sense can't take care of.

There are a few hotels that will not accept children especially some of the higher end boutique B&Bs or lodges. Check in advance.

A good resource is **Kids Friendly New Zealand**, kidsfriendlynz.com. Also, in Queenstown and Wanaka look out for the independent magazine **Kidz Go**, kidz go.co. nz, available from the i-SITE visitor centres.

Customs and immigration

All visitors must have a passport valid for 3 months beyond the date you intend to leave the country. Australian citizens or holders of an Australian returning resident visa can stay in New Zealand indefinitely. UK citizens do not need a visa and are automatically issued with a 6-month visitor permit upon arrival. US, Canadian and other countries with a 'visa waiver' agreement with NZ also do not need a visa for stays of up to 3 months. Other visitors making an application for a visitor permit require: (a) a passport that is valid for at least 3 months after your departure from New Zealand; (b) an onward or return ticket to a country you have permission to enter; (c) sufficient money to support yourself during your stay (approximately NZ$1000 per month).

New Zealand Immigration Service (NZIS) T09-914 4100, T0508-558855, immigration.govt.nz.

Disabled travellers

Most public facilities are well geared up for wheelchairs, however older accommodation establishments and some public transport systems (especially rural buses) are not so well organized. It is a requirement by law to have disabled facilities in new buildings. Most airlines (both international and domestic) are generally well equipped. Disabled travellers usually receive discounts on travel fares and some admission charges. Parking concessions are also available for the disabled and temporary cards can be issued on production of a mobility card or medical certificate.

For more information within New Zealand contact: **New Zealand Disability Resource Centre**, 14 Erson Av, PO Box 24-042 Royal Oak, Auckland, T09-625 8069, disabilityresource.org.nz.

Accessible Kiwi Tours Ltd, T07-362 7622, toursnz.com, is a specialist tour company acting specifically for the disabled, based in Rotorua in the Bay of Plenty.

Emergency

Compared to some countries the average Kiwi 'bobby' is amicable, personable and there to help, not intimidate. For police, fire or ambulance: T111. Make sure you obtain police/medical reports required for insurance claims.

Health

No vaccinations are required to enter the country but you are advised to make sure your tetanus booster is up to date.

The standards of public and private medical care are generally high, but it is important to note that these services are not free. Health insurance is recommended. A standard trip to the doctor will cost around $60 with prescription charges on top of that. Dentists and hospital services are expensive. New Zealand's Accident Compensation Commission (acc.co.nz) provides limited treatment coverage for visitors but it is no substitute for travel/health insurance.

Other than the occasional crazed driver or banking CEO, there are few dangerous creatures in New Zealand with no snakes, crocodiles and so on. Although not poisonous, the dreaded sandfly is common particularly in the wetter and coastal areas of the South Island. These black, pinhead sized 'flying fangs' can annoy you beyond belief. There are numerous environmentally friendly repellents available at pharmacies.

Giardia is a water-borne bacterial parasite on the increase in New Zealand, which, if allowed to enter your system, will cause wall-to-wall vomiting, diarrhoea and rapid weight loss. Don't drink water from lakes, ponds or rivers without boiling it first.

The sun is dangerous and you should take extra care. Ozone depletion is heavy in the more southern latitudes and the incidence of melanomas and skin cancer is above average. Burn times, especially in summer, are greatly reduced so get yourself a silly hat and wear lots of sun block.

New Zealand's weather, especially at higher elevations, is changeable and can be deadly.If you are tramping, or going 'bush' make sure you are properly clothed, take maps, a first-aid kit and a compass. Above all inform somebody of your intentions.

Internet

New Zealand had one of the highest per capita internet access rates in the developed world. Internet cafés and terminals are everywhere and if you are amongst the many who start losing it if you do not get your daily email fix you should be fine. As well as internet cafés, libraries and i-SITES are a good bet, they charge standard rates of $8-$12 per hr. Due to growing competition, rates are getting cheaper, sometimes as little as $3 per hr, but shop around. The website internet-cafe-guide. com is useful for sourcing outlets.

Money

For up-to-date exchange rates, see xe.com.

For international visitors exchange rates are usually in their favour with the euro (2.02), UK£ (2.26) and US$ (1.36) to the New Zealand Dollar NZ$.

The New Zealand currency is the dollar ($), divided into 100 cents (c). Coins come in denominations of 5c, 10c, 20c, 50c, $1 and $2. Notes come in $5, $10, $20, $50 and $100 denominations.

The safest way to carry money is in Traveller's Cheques (TCs). These are available for a small commission from all major banks. American Express (Amex), Visa and Thomas Cook cheques are widely accepted. Most banks do not charge for changing TCs and usually offer the best exchange rates. Keep a record of your cheque numbers and keep the cheques you have cashed separate from the cheques themselves, so that you can get a full refund of all uncashed cheques. It is best to bring NZ$ cheques to avoid extra exchange costs.

All the major credit cards are widely accepted.Most hotels, shops and petrol stations use EFTPOS (Electronic Funds Transfer at Point of Sale), meaning you don't have to carry lots of cash. It is best suited to those who have a bank account in New Zealand, but credit cards can be used with the relevant pin number. If you intend to stay in New Zealand for a while you may be able to open an account with a major bank and secure an EFTPOS/ATM card and PIN. ATMs are readily available in almost all towns and though they accept non-host bankcards, it's best to stick to your own bank's ATMs so you do not incur hidden fees. Credit cards can of course be used and some banks are linked to foreign savings accounts and cards by such networks as Cirrus and Plus.

Almost all towns and villages have at least one of the major bank branches. The main banks are the Bank of New Zealand (BNZ), the National Bank of New Zealand, the ASB Bank, Post Bank and Countrywide Bank with ther trans-Tasman banks, like Westpac Trust and ANZ also in evidence. Bank opening hours are Mon-Fri 0900-1630 with some city branches opening on Sat until 1230. If you need money quickly or in an emergency the best way is to have it wired to you via any major bank with **Western Union** (NZ) T1800- 3256000, westernunion. com; or via **Thomas Cook** and **Moneygram** (NZ) T0800-872893, thomascook.com.

Cost of travelling
For a couple travelling in a campervan, self-catering and eating out occasionally and with an organized mid-range $ activity every 3rd day you will need a minimum of NZ$300 a day. Petrol is not too expensive at around NZ$1.60 per litre (NZ$6 per gallon). It is possible to survive on NZ$80 per person at motor parks with your own jalopy. But that is with no eating out, or activity costs.

Opening hours
Opening times are similar to Europe and the US. In the high season (Nov-Mar) shops generally remain open 7 days a week (0900-1700 or 1730; tourist-oriented outlets often remain open in the evening), banks and post offices open at least Mon-Fri, and 24-hr food stores are common in the main centres.

Post
Post offices (most often called Post Shops) are generally open Mon-Fri 0900-1700, Sat 0900-1230. Within New Zealand standard (local) post costs 50c for medium letters and postcards (2-3 days); $1 for airmail (fast post) to domestic centres (1-2 days); $1.80 for airmail letters to Australia and $1.80 for postcards worldwide and $2.30 for standard overseas airmail letters to Europe, North America, East Asia, Australia and South Pacific. Domestic mail takes 1 to 2 days, perhaps longer in rural areas. When sending any cards or letters overseas be sure to use the free blue 'Air Economy'

stickers. Books of stamps are readily available as are pre-paid envelopes and a range of purpose-built cardboard boxes. Average international delivery times vary depending on the day of the week posted, but a standard letter to the UK can take as few as 4 days (scheduled 6-12 days). North America is scheduled 4-12 days and Australia and the South Pacific 3-8 days. Post Restante services are available in most of the main centres. For details see nzpost.co.nz.

Smoking
It is illegal to smoke in bars, restaurants and the work place, except in the outdoor segregated sections, if provided. Smoking is not allowed on any public transport.

Telephone
The international code for New Zealand is 64. Within New Zealand there are 5 area codes: Auckland and Northland 09; Bay of Plenty, Coromandel, Taupo, Ruapehu and Waikato 07; Eastland, Hawkes Bay, Wanganui and Taranaki 06; Wellington 04; South Island 03. All telephone numbers in this book include the area code.

Telecom payphones are found throughout the country and are colour coded. Although there are both coin (blue) and credit card (yellow) booths available, the vast majority are phone-card only so you are advised to stock up. Cards come in $5, $10, $20 and $50 and are available from many retail outlets, visitor information offices and hostels. Unless you want to see just how fast digital numbers can disappear on screen, do not use these Telecom cards for anything other than domestic calls within New Zealand.

There are a wealth of cheap international calling cards and call centres available. One of the best is **E Phone** eph.co.nz, a calling card that accesses the net through an 0800 number. The cards vary in price from $10-$50 and can be bought from many retail outlets (look for the flag signs outside the shops). They can be used from any landline telephone. Voice instructions will tell you what to do and how much credit you have available before each call.

Local non-business calls are free from standard telephones in New Zealand, so it is not too offensive to ask to use a host's or friend's domestic (non-business) telephone. 0800 or occasionally 0508 precede toll-free calls. Try to avoid 0900 numbers as they are usually very expensive. The 2 major mobile service providers are **Telecom**, telecom.co.nz and **Vodafone**, vodafone.co.nz. Reciprocal arrangements are in place for the use of your own foreign mobile phone, but note these are designed not so much for your convenience as pay for the Telco CEOs latest marvellously facilitated ocean-going mega yacht.

Time difference
New Zealand Standard Time (NZST) is 12 hrs ahead of GMT. From the 1st Sun in Oct to the 3rd Sun in Mar the clock goes forward 1 hr.

Tipping
Tipping in New Zealand is at the customer's discretion. In a good restaurant you should leave a tip of 10-15% if you are satisfied with the service, but the bill may include a service charge. Tipping is appreciated in pubs and bars and taxi drivers also expect some sort of tip; on a longer journey 10% is fine. As in most other countries, hotel porters, bellboys, waiters and waitresses should all be tipped to supplement their meager wages.

Tourist information
The official New Zealand Visitor Information Network is made up of around 100 accredited Visitor Information Centres (VICs) nationally known as i-SITES. Familiarize yourself with the green and black silver fern logo upon arrival.

National i-SITES are based in Auckland and Christchurch as well as the main tourist centres, like Rotorua and Queenstown. Open 7 days a week, they provide a comprehensive information service including accommodation bookings and domestic airline, bus and train ticketing. Souvenir shops and occasionally other retail outlets, currency exchange and cafés are often attached.

Regional i-SITES are found throughout the country and there may be more than one in each region. They provide a general information booking service usually 7 days a week and there is also a huge amount of free material.

Local i-SITES can be found almost anywhere, providing local information as well as assistance in accommodation and transport bookings. They are open at least 5 days a week, but are subject to varying seasonal and weekend hours. For detail refer newzealand.com/travel/i-sites.

Useful websites
For general information start with purenz.com, the official website of the New Zealand Tourism Board. Others include destination-nz.com, searchnz.co.nz and tourism.net.nz. The Department of Conservation website doc.govt.nz provides detailed information on national parks and tramping tracks. For weather, refer to metservice.co.nz and the forecast charts metvuw.com. For New Zealand imagery refer to the author's website darrochdonaldnz.com.

Contents

Footprint features

Auckland, Northland & Coromandel Peninsula

Auckland

With a population of one and a quarter million, Auckland is Polynesia's largest city and by far the biggest in New Zealand. Thanks to its spacious suburban sprawl, Auckland covers more than 500 sq km – twice that of London and close to that of Los Angeles – but because the city is built on an isthmus and constantly fragmented by coastline, you are never far from water. As a result it thankfully lacks that overwhelming sense of humanity over nature. The sea pervades almost every aspect of Auckland life, from recreation to cuisine. Aucklanders own more recreational boats per capita than any other city in the world, earning it the affectionate nicknames of 'City of Sails'. Most sailing is done in Auckland's backyard: the beautiful aquatic playground and island-studded waters of the Hauraki Gulf is one of the most beautiful sailing venues in the world.

For the vast majority of visitors, Auckland will be their arrival point and their first introduction to the country. Many will treat it only as a gateway to better things, but they may be pleasantly surprised by what it has to offer. As well as sailing, you can go fishing, swimming or surfing; all within minutes of the city centre and, in some places, have the beach to yourself. The city also boasts some impressive man-made attractions such as the stunning 360° views from the hypodermic Sky Tower, and its bustling city centre streets and trendy suburbs are home to a thousand quality restaurants.

Arriving in Auckland

Getting there

Airport For airport information refer to aucklandairport.co.nz (T0800-247767). Auckland airport is 21 km southwest of the CBD. Transport to and from the airport is straightforward. The Airbus, T0508-247287, airbus.co.nz, is a cheap option leaving the airport every 20-30 minutes from 0600-2200 (from the city 0435- 2250), $15, child $6 one-way. Taxis wait outside the terminal and charge about $40 to the centre. The Super Shuttle, T0800-748885, supershuttle.co.nz, provides a door-to-door service from $30 one-way. There are no train services.

Bus and train station Train services and most central and suburban buses stop at the Britomart Transport Centre (BBT), centrally located between Customs and Quay streets near the waterfront (bottom of Queen St). Information can be obtained from the terminal itself, all major tourist information offices and by contacting **MAXX** ① *T09-3666400, T0800-103080, maxx.co.nz*. This website also offers a convenient journey planner. The national bus terminal is at the **Sky City Travel Centre** ① *102 Hobson St, Auckland, CBD (below the Sky Tower), T09-583 5780, intercity.co.nz*. Office hours (for sales) daily 0700-1950.

Ferry Almost all ferries depart from the historic Ferry Building on the waterfront, at Quay Street.

Getting around

Bus, train and ferry There are several tourist-oriented passes, a one-day 'Discovery Pass' allowing unlimited travel on bus, ferry and train for $13, or a three-day 'Rover Pass' for $25 that includes the North Shore ferries. The excellent hop-on hop-off Auckland City Loop 'Link' bus (lime green) is an ideal way to get about the city centre and charges a flat fare of $1.60 for each journey. A limited commuter service to some waterside suburbs has been developed, but the vast majority of ferry traffic is tourist-based and operated by **Fullers** ① *T09-367 9111, fullers.co.nz*. There are many excellent island or harbour locations, trips and tours to choose from.

Taxi Typical rates are around $2.75 base charge and then about $2 per kilometre. Taxis are widely available and can be flagged down, ordered by phone or picked up at numerous city centre ranks. Companies include **Auckland Co-Op** ① *T09-300 3000, cooptaxi.co.nz* and **Alert Taxis** ① *T09-309 2000, alerttaxis.co.nz*.

Tourist information

There are visitor information centres (i-SITES) at both airport terminals. There are two main i-SITES in the CBD: Atrium, Sky City, corner Victoria and Federal streets, T09-367 6009, T0800-AUCKLAND, aucklandnz.com, daily 0800-2000; and the quieter Viaduct Harbour, next to the Maritime Museum, corner Quay and Hobson streets, T09-367 6009, November to April daily 0800-1700, May to October 0900-1730. Almost all your mapping needs can be met at **The Auckland Map Centre** ① *National Bank Building, 209 Queen St, T09-309 7725*, and for accommodation booklets and information go to the **AA** ① *99 Albert St, T09-966 8919, aa.co.nz*.

City Centre

Sky Tower, Sky City and the Casino

ⓘ *Corner of Victoria and Federal streets, T0800-759 2489, skycityauckland.co.nz. Observatio* *levels open Sun-Thu 0830-2230, Fri-Sat 0830-2330, \$28, child \$11. Restaurant open lunc* *1000-1500, dinner from 1730, weekend brunch 1000-1500, T09-363 6000. SkyJump/SkyWalk* *T09-368 1835, skyjump.co.nz.*

It took almost three years for the Auckland skyline to sprout its great 328-m hypodermic opening in 1997 to a hail of publicity and – back then – a rather sceptical public. Bu Aucklanders have grown to love their Sky Tower – perhaps because it acts like a beacon and

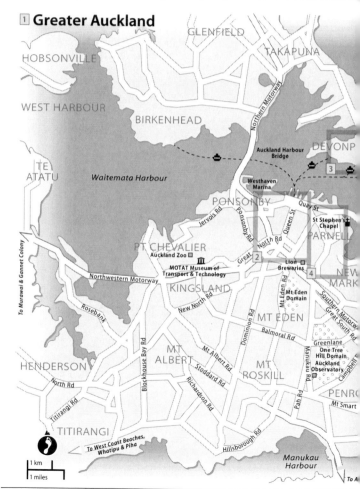

can be seen from miles around. It is indeed an awesome sight and, unless you hate heights, you just have to go up it. As you might expect it has spacious viewing decks and a revolving restaurant from which you can enjoy the 360° views. In recent years, perhaps inevitably, it has also become the focus for some typical Kiwi, lunatic activities including a 192-m controlled bungee known as the 'SkyJump', and the 'SkyWalk' which involves a leisurely stroll round the pergola, with a wee lean over the edge – like you do! (See page 38).

The tower's rather nondescript 'grow-bag' is called Sky City and claims to be Auckland's largest multi-faceted entertainment and leisure destination. The main casino provides all kinds of gambling and gaming options, restaurants, bars and live entertainment 24 hours a day and has no doubt seen the ruin of many and the rapture of few. Even if you are

Sky Tower statistics

The Sky Tower was opened in 1997 and took two years and eight months to build. At 328 m it is the tallest man-made structure in the southern hemisphere. The tower's shaft measures 12 m in diameter and its foundations reach 15 m into the earth. It houses the highest weather station, post box and restaurant in the southern hemisphere. The restaurant completes a 360° revolution every 60 seconds (though six would be far more fun). It is designed to withstand a 8.0 earthquake and 200 kph winds. Such winds would only create a 1-m sway of the entire structure. There are 1257 steps to the Sky Deck. The fastest recorded ascent during the annual 'Sky Tower Vertical Challenge' is five minutes, 57 seconds. In 1998, AJ Hackett made a 192-m bungee jump from the main observation deck, the highest jump ever attempted from a ground structure.

not a gambler it is well worth a look. Less intimidating is the Sky City Theatre, a 700-seat state-of-the-art entertainment venue, staging national and international events and productions. As well as the tower's Orbit restaurant there are five other eateries offering everything from Pacific Rim to Chinese, traditional buffet or café-style options.

Waterfront

Radiating from the historic Ferry Building at the northern end of Queen Street, the waterfront is the place where the city of concrete becomes the City of Sails and where the locals would say it takes on its proper and distinct character. The waterfront has always been a focus of major activity. In the early years it was the point where exhausted immigrants first disembarked to begin a new life in a new land. Later, the immigrant ships gave way to the fleets of log-laden scows bringing kauri to the timber mills. Today, recreation has taken over, as modern ferries come and go, and towards the bridge, lines of expensive yachts rock together at the Westhaven Marina – the largest in the southern hemisphere.

The most rapid development is centered around the Viaduct Basin, which was formerly the hallowed home of the America's Cup Village. When New Zealand took the great yachting cup from the USA's tight grasp in 1995 it became an aquatic stadium of profound celebration.

New Zealand National Maritime Museum (Te Huiteananui-a-Tangaroa)

① *Corner of Quay and Hobson streets, Waterfront, T0800-725897, T09-373 0800, nzmaritime. org. Daily 0900-1700; $17, child $8.50. Guided tours 1030 and 1300. 'Ted Ashby Heritage Cruise' (1½ hrs) in summer Wed-Sun: $29, child $14.50, (includes museum entry).*
Based on the waterfront it depicts a very important aspect of New Zealand's history and the maritime flavour of the City of Sails. Laid out chronologically, you begin with early Maori and Polynesian exploration and arrival before moving through to European maritime history, including immigration. Here, in the replicated living quarters of an early immigrant ship, complete with moving floor and appropriate creaking noises, you cannot help sympathizing deeply with the brave souls who made the journey. It is certainly a long way from sitting back in an Airbus 380 with a gin and tonic, iTunes and the latest Hollywood movie.

Moving on, you emerge into the galleries of New Zealand's proud yachting history, including the stories of New Zealand's participation and triumphs in the Louis Vuitton Cup, the Whitbread Round the World Yacht Race and, of course, the much-lauded Americas Cup. Much of this story is the personal résumé of the late Sir Peter Blake, New Zealand's most famous sailing son who was so tragically murdered in the Amazon in 2002. The centerpiece for the exhibition is the 1995 America's Cup-winning boat NZL32 – Black Magic. The museum also houses a café and shop with nautical gifts and memorabilia.

A number of cruises are also available from the museum, including the popular Ted Ashby Heritage Cruise, aboard the 57-ft traditionally built scow *Ted Ashby* and weekend excursions aboard the unfortunately named but nonetheless charming *SS Puke*. Note you can also experience a cruise on board former Americas Cup yachts with SailNZ (see page 38).

The Domain and Auckland Museum (Te Papa Whakahiku)

ⓘ *T09-3067067, aucklandmuseum.com. Daily 1000-1700, $10 donation. Maori performance Jan-Mar 1100, 1200, 1330, 1430; Apr-Dec 1100, 1200, 1330; $25, child $12.50 (includes entry). Guided tours daily 1030, $10, child $5. Most city tour buses stop at the museum, as does the Link bus from the CBD.*

The **Domain** is one of Auckland's less obvious volcanic cones and New Zealand's oldest park. Originally another enclave and early Maori pa, it was formally put aside as a reserve by Governor Hobson in 1840. Within its spacious grounds are a number of historic and cultural features including the Auckland Museum.

An impressive edifice, the **Auckland Museum** houses some wonderful treasures, displayed with flair and imagination. Its most important collection is that of Maori taonga (treasures) and Pacific artifacts which, combined, is the largest such collection in the world. Other special attractions include an award-winning children's discovery centre, social and settlement history sections, natural history galleries, and 'Scars on the Heart', the story of New Zealanders at war, from the Maori Land Wars in the late 1800s to the campaigns in Gallipoli and Crete in the two world wars of the 20th century. The museum also houses a major national War Memorial.

If you are short of time make sure you see the Maori Court, a fascinating collection of pieces from woven baskets to lethal hand weapons carved from bone or greenstone, all centred round the huge 25-m Te Toki a Tipiri waka (war canoe) and a beautifully carved hotunui (meeting house). A commercial yet entertaining Maori concert is held three to four times daily and guided tours are available. There is a museum café is on the ground floor and a well-stocked museum shop.

Auckland Art Gallery (Toi-o-Tamaki)

ⓘ *Corner of Wellesley and Lorne streets, T09-3791 349, aucklandartgallery.co.nz. Daily 1000-1700, free, $7 for temporary exhibitions; guided tours at 1400. Both galleries are in close proximity and within easy walking distance from Queen St. The Link bus stops right outside the gallery every 10-20 mins.*

The Auckland Art Gallery is essentially two buildings: one in Kitchener Street and the other on the corner of Wellesley Street and Lorne Street in the city centre. They combine to form the largest and most comprehensive collection of art in the country. The first building the Main Gallery (Kitchener Street) is over 100 years old and is currently undergoing major reconstruction. In the meantime the New Gallery (corner of Wellesley and Lorne streets) hosts all current display exhibitions from the permanent collections. These include some of the better-known international masters, particularly 17th-century pieces, but from a national perspective it is the works by Charles Goldie and Gottfried Lindauer that are of particular interest. Goldie and Lindauer were early European settlers who specialized in oil landscapes and portraits of Maori elders in the 18th and 19th centuries. The works of Goldie are impressive to say the least, with their almost Pre-Raphaelite detail bringing the portraits to life, particularly the detail of the moko (Maori facial tattoos).

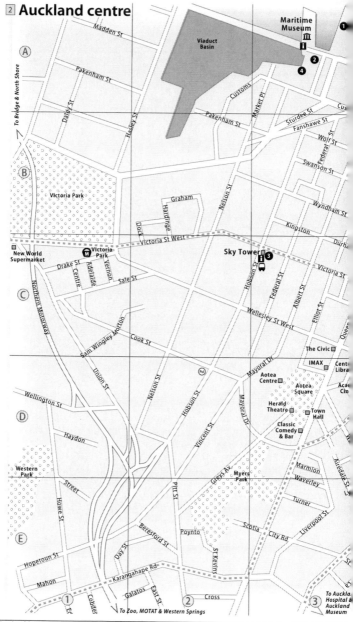

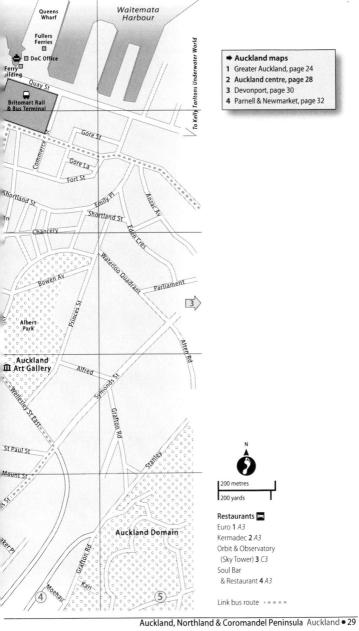

Queens Wharf

Waitemata Harbour

Fullers Ferries

DoC Office

Ferry Building

Quay St

Britomart Rail & Bus Terminal

To Kelly Tarltons Underwater World

Gore St

Commerce St

Gore La

Fort St

Shortland St

Emily Pl

Shortland St

Anzac Av

Chancery

Eden Cres

Waterloo Quadrant

Bowen Av

Parliament

Princes St

Albert Park

Auckland Art Gallery

Alfred

Symonds St

Alten Rd

Wellesley Street E

Grafton Rd

St Paul St

Mount St

Stanley

Auckland Domain

Grafton Rd

Karl

Moehau

➡ Auckland maps
1 Greater Auckland, page 24
2 Auckland centre, page 28
3 Devonport, page 30
4 Parnell & Newmarket, page 32

N

200 metres
200 yards

Restaurants
Euro 1 *A3*
Kermadec 2 *A3*
Orbit & Observatory
 (Sky Tower) 3 *C3*
Soul Bar
 & Restaurant 4 *A3*

Link bus route

Also look out for works by Colin McCahon one of the nation's more contemporary and hugely respected New Zealand artists. **Reuben Cafe** ① *weekdays 0700-1600, Sat/Sun 0900-1530*, is situated next to the New Gallery, with indoor and outdoor seating. Licensed.

City North

Devonport and North Head

① *The waterfront suburb is best accessed by ferry from Quay St, T09-367 9111, fullers.co.nz Mon-Thu every 15 mins 0615-1830, then hourly until 2315, Fri-Sun every 30 mins 0615-0030 last sailing 0100; $11 return, child $5.80. The Devonport i-SITE visitor centre, 3 Victoria St, T09-446 0677, northshorenz.com, daily 0800-1700, can provide information on historic sights, the best short walks and places to stay.*

Devonport's greatest asset is the fact that it is so near yet so far from the city centre, creating a distinct village feel. A 10-minute ferry ride from the city centre brings you immediately to the heart of this historic and picturesque little suburb. Victorian villas, craft shops, pavement cafés and pleasant short walks all lie in wait, dominated by its two extinct volcanoes, Mount Victoria and North Head, both of which offer great views. For a longer stay try one of its many quaint bed and breakfast hideaways or the Esplanade Hotel right on the waterfront.

If time is short your best bet is to take the short walk to North Head, which guards the entrance to Waitemata harbour. Follow the shore east along the pohutukawa-lined King Edward Parade from where you can then climb up and all around North Head and enjoy the commanding views back across the city and the Hauraki Gulf. The warren of underground tunnels and bunkers built amidst the hysteria of various potential invasions during both world wars provide added interest. Cheltenham Beach on the northern side is also a popular swimming and sunbathing spot in summer and one that gives the most

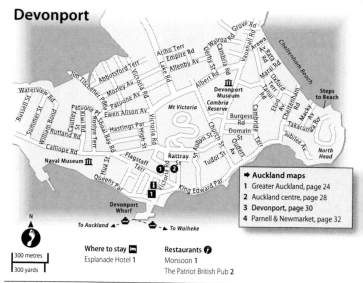

Devonport

➡ Auckland maps
1 Greater Auckland, page 24
2 Auckland centre, page 28
3 Devonport, page 30
4 Parnell & Newmarket, page 32

300 metres
300 yards

Where to stay 🛏
Esplanade Hotel 1

Restaurants 🍴
Monsoon 1
The Patriot British Pub 2

spectacular and almost surreal view of the volcanic island of Rangitoto. On your return to the village, if you are feeling energetic, try to take in more great views from the summit of Mount Victoria.

City East

Mission Bay and Kelly Tarlton's Antarctic Encounter and Underwater World

ⓘ *23 Tamaki Dr, T09-531 5065, kellytarltons.co.nz. Daily 0900-1800, $34, child $17. Kelly Tarlton's operates a free shuttle between Sky City Atrium and Kelly Tarlton's daily between 0900-1700. Or, it is a scenic 6 km walk along the waterfront and Tamaki Drive.*

The first reaction to this attraction is 'Err, so where is it?' The development is actually housed within what used to be Auckland City's sewage holding tanks beneath the car park and Tamaki Drive. It is a fascinating concept, and typical of the imagination, ingenuity and determination of New Zealand's most famous and best-loved diver, treasure hunter and undersea explorer, Kelly Tarlton, the founder and driving force behind the project. Sadly Kelly died just seven months after it opened.

The attraction is divided into three main parts: the Antarctic Encounter; Penguin Encounter; and Underwater World, all of which are pretty self-explanatory, entertaining and informative.

The highlight for many of course are the huge king penguins in their carefully maintained natural conditions. Such is the standard of the facility and the care of the birds that they breed happily and if you are lucky you will see, at close range, the huge and hilarious down-covered chicks.

Tamaki Drive

If you have your own vehicle it is worth continuing east along Tamaki Drive to Mission Bay and St Heliers. On a sunny afternoon, especially at the weekend, there is almost no better place to be in central Auckland than somewhere along Tamaki Drive. All along its 9 km length it is both a buzz of activity and a haven of relaxation. Bike and rollerblade hire is readily available along the route for $8-12 per hour.

Parnell and Newmarket

Trendy Parnell, 2 km east of the city centre, was once a rather run-down suburb, but in recent years it has undergone a dramatic transformation, which has seen it almost overtake Devonport and Ponsonby in the popularity and fashion stakes. It has the same 'village within a city' feel as Devonport, with tiny brick-paved lanes and boutique-style outlets, and boasts some of Auckland's finest galleries, shops and restaurants.

At the top of Parnell Rise is the **Auckland Cathedral of the Holy Trinity** ⓘ *T09-303 9500, holy-trinity.org.nz, Mon-Fri 1000-1600, Sat and Sun 1300-1700, free*, whose angular structure is aesthetically interesting but nothing compared to the beautiful stained-glass windows and 29-ton organ within. Guided tours and an audio-visual display are both available.

South of the cathedral, Parnell merges into the more modern commercial centre and suburb of Newmarket, which is best known for its shops, restaurants, cafés and entertainment venues.

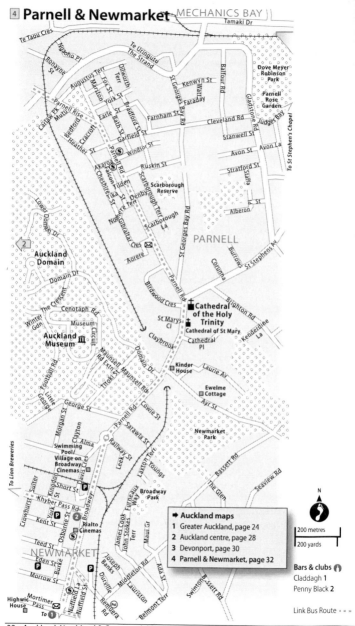

Auckland maps
1 Greater Auckland, page 24
2 Auckland centre, page 28
3 Devonport, page 30
4 Parnell & Newmarket, page 32

200 metres
200 yards

N

Bars & clubs
Claddagh 1
Penny Black 2

Link Bus Route • • •

City West and South

Auckland Zoo

ⓘ *Motions Rd, Western Springs, T09-360 3819, aucklandzoo.co.nz. Daily 0930-1730, $22, child $11, 5 mins' drive from the centre; from the Great Western Motorway take the Western Springs off ramp and follow signs, free car parking. Or take Explorer Bus or Bus 045 from the city centre.*

Set in pleasant parkland next to Western Springs and 6 km west of the city centre is New Zealand's premier wild animal collection. It has kept pace with the more conservation-minded function of zoos and is worth a visit. The zoo claims to be leading the way in the breeding of native species including kiwi and tuatara – both of which are on display. All the old favourites are also there – elephants (sometimes taken on walkabout around the zoo), giraffes, hippos, tigers and orangutans. Auckland Zoo has gradually developed some imaginative themed exhibits over the years, including the Newstalk ZB Rainforest where you feel more captive than the obscenely laid-back spider monkeys; Pridelands, the spacious home of the giraffe, lion and zebra with its adjoining Hippo River and Sealion Shores, a new state-of-the-art pinniped exhibit. KidZone provides the usual touchy-feelies with rabbits and other assorted furry friends. Several tours are also offered including the increasingly popular behind-the-scenes animal encounters, from $150, T09-360 4700.

Mount Eden

At 196 m, Mount Eden is the closest dormant volcano to the city centre providing great city views. The best time to come here is at dawn, especially on misty winter mornings, when it can be a photographer's delight, and you can avoid the coach-loads of visitors. At the southern base of the mount, **Eden Gardens** ⓘ *24 Omana Av, T09- 6388395, edengarden. co.nz, daily 0900-1630, $8, child free, concessions available, café 1000-1600*, is a great place for lovers of all things green that grow. Mount Eden is a long walk from the city centre, and given the climb you might be better off taking Bus 274 or 275 from the BBT in the CBD.

Cornwall Park and One Tree Hill

ⓘ *Cornwall Park visitor centre, T09-630 8485, cornwallpark.co.nz. Open 1000-1600, free. Café and free trail leaflet.*

Just to the south of Mount Eden is Cornwall Park, famous not only for its crowning glory, the monument and the tree, but also the well preserved remains of a Maori pa on and around the summit. Kiwi Tamaki, the great chief of the Nga Marama, lived here during the mid-18th century with his thousands of whanau (family) and followers, attracted by the rich pickings of the region's coast and its fertile soils. His claim to the region ended after being routed by sub-tribes from the north and his people being decimated by a smallpox epidemic introduced by the Europeans. It was the Scot, Logan Campbell, the most powerful and well known of the new capital's residents, who eventually took ownership. Shortly before his arrival, a single Totara tree stood proudly on the summit. This had already given rise to the hill's Maori name, Te-Totara-a-Ahuameaning 'Hill of the single Totara'. Early settlers rudely cut down this tree in 1852 and it was Campbell who planted several trees in its place, including the lonesome pine you could see from miles around, until its demise in 2001.

At the base of the hill is a visitor centre in **Huia Lodge**, Campbell's original gatekeeper's house. It houses some interesting displays. Across the road is the simple and faithfully restored **Acacia Cottage** in which Campbell himself lived, though the building itself originally stood in the city centre and was relocated here in the 1920s.

Also within the park boundary at its southern end is the **Auckland Observatory** ① *Manakau Rd, T09-6241246, stardome.org.nz, times and events vary; standard viewing sessio with show $16, child $8.* This is the official home of Auckland's stargazers, and also contain the Stardome Planetarium, a cosmic multimedia experience played out on the ceiling fo the general public. Outdoor telescope viewing sessions and special events are also held depending on what the weather and the heavens are up to. You can even adopt a star a interesting concept that will probably have you trying to find it again, for the rest of your life

Around Auckland

Though you are doubtless like a sheepdog on a lead, just dying to be let off on your New Zealand adventure proper, bear in mind the Auckland region has much to offer beyond the suburbs and still within view of its mighty Sky Tower. Take a day or two to explore the myriad islands or rugged West Coast beaches and it will be time well spent. Your sense of the city will almost certainly change. Here you begin to realize how New Zealand's remarkable natural assets pervade everything, even a city of over one million people.

Waitakere and the West Coast
Waitakere City West Auckland, or Waitakere City, is made up of a number of diverse suburbs of little note the tourist. At the fringe of the city is the pleasant little village suburb of Titirangi, which serves 'the gateway to the Waitakeres. The 'Waitaks', as they are affectionately known, are one of the region's biggest and most attractive regional parks offering a 200-km network of walking tracks, many of which hide such scenic delights as large kauri trees, waterfalls and large dams. Before embarking on any outdoor activities in the area, visit the **Arataki Information Centre** ① *on the hill at the southern end of Scenic Dr, 6 km from Titirangi, T09-817 0089, T09-817 0077, arc.govt.nz, daily 0900-1700, 1600 in winter.* Dominating its façade is an impressive Maori pou (carving), which lost its manhood a few years ago (though another was duly carved, and the glint in his little paua shell eye restored). Inside there are interpretative displays and all the information you will need about the area and its natural history.

Hellaby House ① *515 Scenic Dr, gardens. Mon-Sat 1300-1600, Sun 1100-1700, free.* If you are limited for time and do not intend to visit the west coast beaches you should at least take the 28-km Scenic Drive that winds its way along the eastern fringe of the Waitakeres. It offers views across the city both by day and by night, with one of the best vantage points being from the garden of Hellaby House, just below the TV masts.

Wineries West Auckland is also one of the lesser-known wine-producing areas of the country, containing nearly 20 wineries with such famous names as Corbans, Coopers Creek and Nobilo. The northern areas of Waitakere City host most of these, especially in the Kumeu area. Most wineries offer tastings. Copies of the official Wine Trail and Wineries of Auckland leaflets can be secured at the main city i-SITES.

West Coast beaches Wineries and Waitaks aside, what really draws people west are the wild west coast beaches at Whatipu, Kare Kare, Piha, Bethells and Muriwai. The most popular and accessible of these is the coastal enclave of Piha, with its excellent (yet dangerous) surf breaks and fishing spots. Muriwai Beach (the most northerly) also hosts a breeding colony of gannets viewable from an observation deck.

But if you have time and fancy real solace, then head south to Whatipu, or north to ethells, where a stroll along the beach will give you – perhaps for the first time – a sense f what New Zealand is all about. Welcome, at last to the nature made New Zealand, as pposed to the man-made. From here on it just gets better and better!

auraki Gulf Islands

or general information contact the **Auckland (i-SITE) visitor centre** ① *137 Quay St, Princes Vharf, Downtown, T09-3796476.* The Hauraki Gulf is famed for its picturesque islands, vhich range in size from the 179-ha Motuihe to the 93-sq-km Waiheke. There is significant ontrast in their use and character as well as their geography.

There is no doubt that given a few days in Auckland you should visit at least one island. Vhich one really comes down to your interests beyond just pure aesthetics as all offer jreat views and beaches. If you are a wine lover then it would be rude not to visit Waiheke is it is home to some of the finest labels in the country including Goldwater Estate and Stonyridge. For walking, views and geological interest, let alone sheer convenience, head or Rangitoto. For wildlife there is no doubt Tiritiri Matangi offers a superb day out, while or a true island adventure take a few days to explore the wilds of Great Barrier.

Waiheke ① *Contact Fullers Ferries, Ferry Building, Quay St, T09-367 9111, fullers.co.nz. Fares rom $35. For tourist information contact the Waiheke i-SITE visitor centre, 2 Korora Rd, in ront of the Artworks Complex, Oneroa, T09-372 1234, Mon-Sun 0900-1700, waihekenz.com, ourismwaiheke.co.nz and gotowaiheke.co.nz.* Close to the city, Waiheke is by far the most populated, so much so that it is often labeled 'just another suburb' of Auckland. Famed for its vineyards and blessed with a number of fine beaches, it has for decades been a avourite and convenient escape from the city for both residents and visitors.

Rangitoto ① *Contact Fullers Ferries, Ferry Building, Quay St, T09-367 9111, fullers.co.nz. Fares from $27.* Perhaps most obvious among the island family is Rangitoto with its atypical volcanic cone that dominates the horizon and although now fully clad in bush reveals some fascinating lava flows upon closer inspection via a network of walking tracks.

Great Barrier ① *Contact Fullers Ferries, Ferry Building, Quay St, T09-367 9111, fullers.co.nz. Fares from $130.* Sealink (Subritzky Shipping), T0800-732546, T09-300 5900, sealink.co.nz, offer a vehicle (and passenger) service from 45 Jellicoe St, Freemans Bay, Auckland, but it is expensive. Note you can hire vehicles or take organized tours on the island. By air contact Great Barrier Airlines, Auckland Domestic Terminal (and at the airfield on the Barrier at Claris), T09-275 9120, T0800-900600, greatbarrierairlines.co.nz. From $109 one-way. Fly/cruise packages are also available, from $169. For tourist information the i-SITE Visitor Centre is in the post shop in Claris, T09-429 0033, T09-367 6009, greatbarrier.co.nz, daily 0900-1700. Also useful is greatbarrierisland.co.nz. The second largest island in the group, Great Barrier, is 90 km from the city, and offers a true island escape and some superb scenery, walks and beaches.

Tiritiri Matangi ① *Contact 360-Discovery, T0800-3603472, T09-307 8005, 360discovery. co.nz.* Runs a service from Auckland from Pier 4, Wed to Sun at 0900, $66, child $29; or the same ferry from Z Pier, Gulf Harbour on the Whangaparaoa Peninsula, 50 mins later, $49, child $24.50. Trips return by 1600. For tourist information refer to tiritirimatangi.org.nz. Two other islands in the Hauraki are the world-renowned wildlife reserves of Tiritiri Matangi near the Whangaparaoa Peninsula on the city's northern fringe, and the mountainous Little

Barrier, which can be seen on a clear day to the north. Tiri is the most accessible and offers visitors an insight into what New Zealand used to be like, with abundant bird life and such enchanting avian odysseys as the takahe and spotted kiwi. Little Barrier is home to a few precious and well-looked-after kakapo – a large flightless parrot that with less than 100 remaining is one of the rarest birds in the world.

Auckland listings

For hotel and restaurant price codes and other relevant information, see pages 9-14.

🛏 Where to stay

Auckland *p22,*
maps p24, p28, p30 and p32
$$$$-$$$ Esplanade Hotel, 1 Victoria Rd, Devonport, T09-445 1291, esplanade hotel.co.nz. One of Auckland's oldest hotels, dominating the promenade with fine views of the harbour. Due to its position (15 mins from the city centre by car, or a 10-min ferry ride from the CBD) it's a good place to get away from the centre and enjoy Devonport's 'village within a city' atmosphere. All rooms are en suite, with the spacious harbour view suites being the most sought after. Sky TV and Wi-Fi. Classy in-house restaurant with an open fire in winter adds to the charm. Tariff includes breakfast.
$$$ Great Ponsonby B&B, 30 Ponsonby Terr, Ponsonby, T09-376 5989, greatpons. co.nz. Undoubtedly one of the best in the city, this B&B is a restored villa in a quiet location only a short stroll to the funky Ponsonby Road. Range of tastefully decorated en suite rooms and studios with a colourful Pacific influence. Enthusiastic, knowledgeable owners and a friendly dog and cat. The fantastic breakfasts are all cooked to order, using only fresh ingredients.

Motor parks
$$$-$ Manukau Top Ten Holiday Park, 902 Great South Rd, Manukau City, T09-266 8016, manukautop10.co.nz. Handy for the airport or for those heading south.
$$$-$ North Shore Motels and Top Ten Holiday Park, 52 Northcote Rd, Takapuna,

T09-418 2578, nsmotels.co.nz. The most popular holiday park in the city but around 35 km from the airport, offering lodges, motel and cabin accommodation as well as the usual reliable Top Ten motor camp facilities. 5 mins to the beach.

🍴 Restaurants

Auckland *p22,*
maps p24, p28, p30 and p32
$$$ Euro, Shed 22, Princes Wharf, Quay St, T09-309 9866. Daily for lunch and dinner, brunch Sat-Sun from 1030. A waterfront restaurant designed to capture the sailing crowd, with a boast of being the 'best of the best'. It has a very luxurious interior with a large mesmerizing clock projected onto the wall, and offers new and imaginative cuisine in the revered Pacific Rim style. Licensed, outdoor dining available.
$$$ Kermadec, 1st floor, Viaduct Quay Building, corner of Lower Hobson St and Quay St, T09-3090412, kermadec.co.nz. Mon-Fri for lunch and dinner. Perhaps the best restaurant in town, and arguably the best seafood venue. Tickle your taste buds with the many delights of the Pacific Ocean as well as more traditional fare. There are 2 private rooms in a Japanese-style decor that contain small ponds. Don't miss the seafood platter. Licensed and BYO.
$$$-$$ Orbit Restaurant, Sky Tower, corner Victoria St and Federal St, T09-363 6000. Brunch Sat/Sun 1000-1500, lunch Mon-Fri 1130-1430, dinner daily 1730-2230, lunch Thu-Sun. More than two-thirds of the way up the Sky Tower, this restaurant has the best view of any in the city, if not the entire hemisphere. The restaurant itself

evolves of course, apparently once every ~~r~~, though every 6 secs would be far more ~~un~~. Contemporary Pacific-rim cuisine and ~~xtensive~~ NZ wine list. The Observatory is ~~he~~ other option in the Sky Tower and offers ~~uffet~~-style fare. Licensed.

$$ Ponsonby Fresh Fish and Chip Co, ~~27~~ Ponsonby Rd, Ponsonby, T09-378 7885. ~~D~~aily 1100-2130. A Ponsonby institution. ~~A~~lthough the portions have gradually ~~d~~ecreased in size, the quality has pretty ~~m~~uch stayed the same. Try the local Pacific ~~f~~ish. Always busy, and it is takeaway only, so ~~e~~xpect to place an order then return about ~~2~~0 mins later. Good vegetarian burgers.

$$ Soul Bar and Restaurant, Viaduct ~~H~~arbour, T09-356 7249, soulbar.co.nz. Daily ~~f~~or lunch and dinner. Much to the chagrin ~~o~~f the local competition, owner and chef ~~J~~udith Tabron ensured that Soul was the ~~p~~lace to be during the America's Cup and ~~i~~ts reputation lives on. Doubtless, the open-~~a~~ir decks overlooking the harbour had ~~m~~uch to do with that and of course the bar ~~i~~s the main attraction, but the food is also ~~e~~xcellent and affordable. Internationally ~~r~~enowned guest chefs add to its appeal.

$$ The Patriot British Pub, 14 Victoria ~~R~~d, Devonport, T09-445 3010. Sure, 'When ~~i~~n Rome…' as the saying goes, but if you ~~a~~re European and weary of all things new, ~~w~~ant a good beer, or a hearty breakfast or rapport with ex-pats then head here on a sunny Sun or weekend evening.

$$-$ Dizengoff, 256 Ponsonby Rd, Ponsonby, T09-360 0108. Daily 0700-1700. A quintessential Auckland café that attracts a wide-ranging clientele, making it a great spot for people watching. The breakfasts (especially the salmon and eggs on toast) are delicious. Unlicensed.

🎭 Entertainment

Auckland *p22*,
maps p24, p28, p30 and p32
For the latest live music, theatre and cinema listings for Auckland check the daily and especially the weekend *New Zealand Herald*, nzherald.co.nz, or *eventsauckland.com* and *nzlive.com*. The free publication *What's Happening* is also a very useful guide, and is available from the visitor information centre. For ticketing and nationwide entertainment listings refer to the online service ticketek, ticketek.co.nz. For Festivals, see page 16.

The Edge, T0800-289842, the-edge.co.nz. A conglomerate of Auckland's main venues offering the top international performance events. It combines the Aotea Centre, The Civic, the Auckland Town Hall, and Aotea Square. The event schedule leaflets are available from all the main information centres.

Sky City, T0800-7592489, skycityauckland. co.nz. The cinemas are at Sky City Metro, 291-297 Queen St, T09-979 2400. The largest entertainment venue in Auckland with its showpiece casino (open 24 hrs), but there is plenty more with a theatre and a 12-screen cinema.

🛍 Shopping

Auckland *p22*,
maps p24, p28, p30 and p32
If you are looking for products specific to New Zealand, whet your appetite by visiting the **New Zealand Trade Centre**, 26 Albert St, Auckland City, T09-366 6879, nztc.co.nz. Although you cannot actually buy things here, it will give you an insight into what is available.

Otara Market, Otara town centre car park, 18 km south of the city centre, T09-274 0830. Every Sat 0600-1100. Thought to be the largest Maori/Polynesian market in the world.

Victoria Park Market, opposite Victoria Park, just a few mins' walk west of the city centre, victoria-park-market.co.nz. It provides 7 days a week shopping with a variety of outlets from shops to stalls that expand into the car park on Sat. There are a wide variety of products with a market theme, a number of good cafés, a food hall and a pub, all in pleasant surroundings.

● What to do

Auckland *p22,*
maps p24, p28, p30 and p32
Bungee and sky jumping
Bridge Climb and Bungee, Harbour Bridge
Experience (Bridge Climb), Westhaven
Reserve, T09-360 7748, ajhackett.com.
1½ hrs from $120. Bungee $150. The
Auckland Harbour Bridge has – not
surprisingly – been utilized by Mr Hackett
for both bungee and bridge climb. The
verdict? If you are going to Sydney this
is of course nothing compared to their
Harbour Bridge walk, also if you are going
to Queenstown, save your money until
then. Otherwise go for it!
Sky Jump and Sky Walk, T0800-759586,
skyjump. co.nz. From $225 (maximum
weight 125 kg). This is the original and
much-talked about jump from just above
the restaurant of the Sky Tower. But there
is a catch (thankfully, or sadly, depending
how you look at it). Given the incredible
jump height of 192 m, not to mention
the surroundings, it is not possible to
jump conventionally with an elastic cord
attached to the ankles and to do the yoyo
bit. Obviously if you did, in this scenario,
you would probably end up plastered
against somebody's window. That said, at
20 secs and 75 kph it is should still get the
adrenaline-pumping. Sky Walk is the latest
Sky Tower adventure that involves walking
around the tower's pergola (or ring) on a
1-m walkway with 192-m drop and nothing
but thin air on either side. An overhead
safety tether travels above. Look and Leap,
a Skyjump and Skywalk combo, costs $290.

Cruises and sailing
360-Discovery Cruises, T0800-888006,
360discovery.co.nz. Offer a range of
harbour cruise options as well as day trips
to Kawau Island, Tiritiri Matangi and the
Coromandel Peninsula.
Explore NZ, T09-359 5987, sailnz.co.nz.
Offer excellent sailing trips as well as whale
and dolphin viewing and swimming. Their
SailNZ operation offers basic cruises on, or
match races between authentic Americas
Cup racing yachts, the NZL 40 and NZL 41,
from $160 (racing from $210, child $180).
Fullers, Fullers Cruise Centre, Ferry Building
waterfront, T09-367 9111, fullers.co.nz.
The main ferry operator offering everything
from 2-hr harbour cruises to island
transportation and stopovers. They can
also arrange wine tours of Waiheke.

Tours
Potiki Adventures, T021-422773,
potikiadventures.co.nz. Excellent Maori-
themed adventure tours, with a range of
fixed or custom activities from hiking to
marae stays. Their Auckland Orientation Trip
is a fine introduction to the city, region and
country from the Maori perspective.

● Transport

Auckland *p22,*
maps p24, p28, p30 and p32
See Arriving in Auckland, page 23.

● Directory

Auckland *p22,*
maps p24, p28, p30 and p32
Hospital Auckland Hospital, Park Rd,
Grafton, T09-3670000.

Northland

Northland is often called the 'birthplace of the nation' as it was here that the first Maori set foot in New Zealand, about AD 800, followed by the first European settlers over 800 years later. It was also here, in the Bay of Islands in 1840, that the Treaty of Waitangi was signed – the document that launched the relationship between two deeply contrasting peoples. This relationship is reflected in the calms and the storms of unsettled ocean currents that unite uneasily at New Zealand's northernmost point, Cape Reinga. Elsewhere, lost in time within the Waipoua Forest, making all that human history seem like yesterday, stands one of the few remaining ancient kauri trees: the centuries-old Tane Mahuta.

All in all, for the modern-day visitor, Northland must feature as one of the most aesthetically and historically interesting regions to visit in New Zealand and although psychologically, given that there is such a pull to the south, it may seem heading to Northland is the wrong thing to do, if time allows you will certainly congratulate yourself on the decision to go and on your sense of non-conformity.

Warkworth and the Kowhai Coast

Visiting Warkworth and the Kowhai Coast Warkworth is 68 km north of Aucklanc Whangarei 162 km and Paihia 233 km on SH1. Regional buses serve all the main centre with the principal operator being **Intercity** (Northliner) ① *T09-583 5780, intercity.co.n* There is no rail service. **Bay of Islands i-SITE visitor centre** ① *The Wharf, Marsden R* Paihia, T09-4027345, T0800-363463, visitnorthland.co.nz.* **Whangarei i-SITE visitor centr** ① *Tarewa Park, 92 Otaika Rd, Whangarei, T09-438 1079, whangareinz.org.nz.* **Warkwort** i-SITE visitor centre ① *1 Baxter St, Warkworth, T09-425 9081, warkworthnz.com.*

Although not geographically within Northland, Warkworth is for most a starting point anc a gateway to the region. Most travellers, in their haste to reach the Bay of Islands, mis it out altogether, while others take the slower and more scenic route north, along the Kowhai Coast, via the vineyards of Matakana, then on to the scenic coastal settlements o Leigh, Mangawhai and Waipu. Whatever your intention, if you have time Warkworth anc the pleasant coastal bays, peninsulas and islands to its east are certainly worthy of a stop.

About 4 km north of Warkworth is **Sheepworld** ① *T09-425 7444, sheepworldfarm.co.nz* daily 0900-1700, shows at 1100 and 1400, $12, with show $26, child $10, and if the foo falls heavy on the accelerator at the very prospect of such a place, then just hold off. It i actually quite entertaining and worthy of the stop. Kids are allowed to feed the lambs and you can get involved in some shearing. There is also a café – 'The Black Sheep.'

The countryside around Matakana, 8 km north of Warkworth on the main Warkworth tc Leigh Road is increasingly famous for its vineyards. The i-SITE visitor centre in Warkworth can provide full wine trail details.

Further east other areas worth investigating are the **Tawharanui** (pronounced 'Ta-fara-nui') **Coastal Park** and the **Goat Island Marine Reserve** ① *near Leigh, T09-422 6334, glassbottomboat.co.nz.* Tawharanui is quieter than most other parks and offers great beaches, walks and scenery, while at Goat Island you can view the assorted and colourful sea life by glass-bottom boat.

Waipu

Labelled by many a kiwi kid as 'Whynot', poor Waipu does suffer a bit from its name. But what does Waipu really mean? It is Maori, of course: wai (water) and pu (song).

Waipu was founded in 1853 by a party of 120 Scottish settlers who were part of a group of 400 that originally left their homelands under the resolute leadership of the Reverend Norman McLeod. They did so in desperation during the terrible Highland Clearances, which resulted in mass migrations in the early 1800s. The small community is very proud of its Scottish heritage and no visit to Waipu would be complete without a look inside the **Waipu Museum and Heritage Centre** ① *T09-432 0746, waipumuseum.com, 0930-1630, $8, child $6.* The museum walls are decked with photographs, and faces of early immigrants look down on cases full of personal effects from spectacles to spinning wheels. Logbooks listing the immigrant arrivals and the ships on which they arrived are being continuously updated and it really is a fascinating place.

Every New Year's Day since 1871 the Waipu Highland Games – the largest and longest-running in the southern hemisphere – gets into full swing with highland dancers, pipe bands and of course, kilted caber-tossers.

Whangarei

Given the obvious allure of the Bay of Islands to the north, with its promise of stunning scenery and a whole host of activities, few visitors pay much attention to Northland's largest town. However, if you do choose to linger here a while, you will find that it has a lot to offer.

Town Basin is an award-winning development that hosts a number of museums and galleries including the **Clapham's Clock Museum** ① *T09-438 3993, claphamsclocks. com, daily 0900-1700, $8, child $4*, home to the biggest collection of timepieces in the southern hemisphere.

In the suburb of Maunu, 6 km west of town (SH14) is the **Whangarei Museum, Clarke Homestead and Kiwi House** ① *T09-438 9630, whangareimuseum.co.nz, daily 1000-1600, $15, $5 all sites*. It is an indoor/outdoor complex known collectively as Kiwi North with a colonial farming block and homestead and a modern building housing a number of taonga or Maori treasures, including a musket that belonged to the great northern warrior Hone Heke. The Kiwi House is one of the better examples in the country.

East of the city at Whangarei Heads is **Ocean Beach** one of Northland's finest: it's quiet, beautiful and, in a raging easterly wind, a place where the senses are bombarded with nature at its best. On the way you will begin to notice the prevalence of evocative Scots place names like McLeod's and Urquhart's Bay; all family names of the overspill Scots settlers from the Waipu enclaves.

Tutukaka Coast

Even if fishing and scuba-diving did not exist, the Tutukaka coastline would still deserve to be one of the finest coastal venues in Northland. But its rugged scenic bays are best known throughout New Zealand and beyond as the gateway and safe harbour to some of the best deep-sea fishing and diving in the world. **The Poor Knights Islands**, which lie 25 km offshore, are internationally significant both above and below the waterline, with a wide range of wildlife and vegetation. Most activity in the area takes place from Tutukaka with its large sheltered marina while the village of Ngunguru, 5 km before it, has most of the visitor and resident amenities. For dive operators, see page 52.

2 Whangarei centre

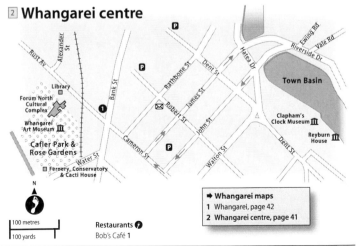

➡ Whangarei maps
1 Whangarei, page 42
2 Whangarei centre, page 41

100 metres
100 yards

Restaurants 🍴
Bob's Café 1

☐ Whangarei

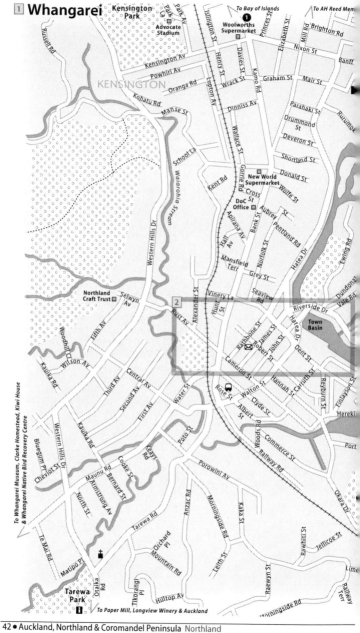

➡ **Whangarei maps**
1 Whangarei, page 42
2 Whangarei centre, page 41

kaka Coast, Whangarei Falls

Mt Parahaki
(241m)

Memorial Dr

To Abbey Caves

11 Punga
Grove
Av

Kohe St

Bahama Pl

Jessie St

Memorial Dr

Panorama Dr

Kauri Pl

Riverside Dr

Tanekaha Dr

To Airport

N

300 metres
300 yards

Where to stay 🛏
Whangarei Top Ten Holiday Park 1

Restaurants 🍴
A Deco 1

Waioneone Creek

ne Burners
Creek

Hundertwasser WC

You might think it ridiculous to recommend a public convenience as a major attraction but if you have time, visit the Kawakawa 'Hundertwasser' Public Toilets in the centre of Kawakawa, 17 km south of Paihia. This marvellous and colourful creation of local artist Friedrich Hundertwasser who died in 2000, is now something of an icon and a monument.

The Bay of Islands

Paihia is the main launching point for the Bay of Islands yet strangely upon arrival by road all you can see is one very little island just offshore. But, they are out there – all 150 of them. The Bay of Islands is one of the major tourist draws in the country, offering the visitor numerous water-based activities and superb coastal scenery. The area is also of huge historic significance in that it is the site of the first European settlement and the signing of the Treaty of Waitangi – the document that began the uneasy voyage of New Zealand's bicultural society. While the islands themselves are the main attraction, most are uninhabited and you can only stay at designated campsites. Most visitors stay on the mainland and take cruises to the islands. You can also explore them by kayak, yacht or sailing boat; go big-game fishing for marlin or shark; dive amidst shoals of blue maomao; swim with the dolphins; bask in the sun; or jump out of a plane.

Paihia was the site of New Zealand's first church and missionary centre, but unless you have an inexplicable fetish for motels there is little in the way of sights, with the town acting primarily as an accommodation and amenity centre for tourists.

Most people take SH1 to the Bay of Islands, though a far more interesting route is via the Old Russell Road which leaves SH1 for the coast at Whakapara, about 26 km north of Whangarei. Welcome to rural Northland and the simple spirit of the north.

Waitangi National Reserve
① *T09-402 7437, waitangi.net.nz. Daily 0900-1700. $25, child $12.*
This is the heart of New Zealand's historical beginnings and a rather politically correct outline of events that led to the signing of the Treaty of Waitangi in 1840 and the significance of the document right up to the present day. The main focus of the reserve is the beautifully restored **Treaty House**, built in 1833-1834 and once home of British resident, James Busby, who played a crucial role in the lead-up to the treaty signing. The house is full of detailed and informative displays that help clarify the quite confusing series of events surrounding the creation of the treaty. Near the Treaty House the reserve boasts perhaps the most visited **Whare Runanga** (Maori meeting house) in the country. To call this, or any whare merely a house is rather an understatement. They are essentially artworks, with all the meaning, soul and effort therein and the Whare Runanga at Waitangi is a fine example.

From the Whare Runanga it is a short walk down to the shore where the **war canoe** Ngatokimatawhaorua is housed. This 35-m-long craft is named after the canoe in which Kupe, the Maori ancestor and navigator, discovered Aotearoa (New Zealand), and is launched every year as part of the Waitangi Day commemoration ceremonies hosted on and around the national reserve.

There are regular 30-minute Maori performances. Another addition to the Waitangi experience is the **Culture North Treaty of Waitangi Night Show** ① *T09-4025990,*

Paihia & Waitangi

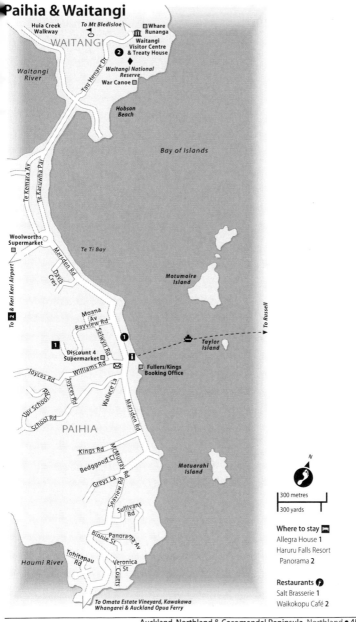

culturenorth.co.nz, $65 all-inclusive, free pick-up, which is staged most evenings in summer and is recommended. It is genuine and so far lacking in the commercialism so rife in other tourist areas. This is the one must-do beyond the islands themselves.

Russell

① *Russell can be reached by passenger ferry from Paihia Wharf, Oct-Mar every 30 mins 0720-2230, $6, child $3, or there is a vehicle ferry every 10 mins from Opua, 9 km south of Paihia, daily 0650-2200, car and driver $10, campervan $16, passenger $1, all one-way.*

About 2 km across the bay from Paihia, yet still on the mainland, is the settlement of Russell. It enjoys a village feel and a rich history that eludes its frenetic, tourism-based neighbour. With the advent of the first European settlement, Kororareka quickly grew to be the base for whalers, sealers and escaped convicts and earned the sordid and notorious reputation as 'the hellhole of the Pacific'. The earliest missionaries tried their best to quell the unholy mob with mixed results. When the Treaty of Waitangi was signed in 1840, although it was the largest European settlement in New Zealand, William Hobson, the then governor, decided it was not a good marketing ploy to give it capital status and instead bought land in what is now Auckland. To make matters worse, the treaty was seen by local Maori as a fraud and not as beneficial as was promised, with financial benefits in particular failing to materialize. Their scorn (led by the infamous chief Hone Heke) was focused on the Flagstaff near Russell, which proudly flew the Union Jack. Heke and his men duly cut it down, not once, but four times after which Kororareka was sacked and the first Maori Wars began. Once relative peace returned the authorities decided to make a new beginning and lose the notorious label, calling it Russell.

Today Russell, along with Kerikeri, is flaunted as the most historic village in New Zealand. The **Russell Museum** ① *2 York St, T09-4037701, russellmuseum.org.nz, daily 1000-1700, $7.50, child $2*, has an interesting collection of early settler relics and, having being built to commemorate the bicentenary of Captain Cook's visit in 1769, features a host of information about the explorer including an impressive model of Cook's ship, *Endeavour*.

A short distance along the shore from the museum is **Pompallier House** ① *T09-403 9015, daily 1000-1700, $7.50, child $3.50*. It is New Zealand's oldest surviving Roman Catholic building, built in 1842 as the printery, tannery and storehouse for the French Marist mission at Kororareka.

On the corner of Church Street and Robertson Street is the 1836 **Anglican Church**, which was one of the few buildings to survive the 1840s sacking and Maori war (bar a few visible musket ball holes) and remains the oldest church in New Zealand. For a grand view it is worth the steep climb to Flagstaff Hill (Maiki). Parts of the current pole were erected in the late 1850s over a decade after Hone Heke's admirable attempts at clear felling.

One kilometre north, the earth terraces of the ancient pa on the **Tapeka Point Reserve** make a pleasant walk, while **Long Beach**, 1 km behind the village, is also a pleasant spot and a fine venue on a hot summer's day.

Kerikeri

Travelling north from Paihia the rolling hills give way to corridors of windbreaks that hide the laden trees of citrus, grape and kiwifruit for which the area is famous. The word *keri* means 'dig', and it was here, in pleasant little Dig Dig, that the first plough cut into New Zealand soil in 1820. Along with Russell, Kerikeri is rich in Maori and early European history with the **Kerikeri Basin**, 2 km northeast of the present town, being the nucleus of New Zealand's first European colonization.

For a sense of history and atmosphere head straight for the Basin past the main commercial centre. There the road falls to meet the babbling Kerikeri River and the dominant and attractive **Stone Store** ① *daily 1000-1700, $3.50*. This was New Zealand's first stone building and was completed in 1835. The first Anglican bishop George Selwyn used it as a library in the early 1840s and later as an ammunition store during conflicts between Ngapuhi chief Hone Heke, before assuming its intended purpose as a general mission store. Today it is neatly laid out as testimony to that function with a museum on its top floor.

Almost immediately next door is the two-storey Kemp House or **Mission House** ① *daily 1000-1700, $5, combined entry with Stone Store $7.50, children free*. This is the oldest surviving building in New Zealand (at the very young age of 188). It was established by pioneer missionary Samuel Marsden on land offered to him by the great local Maori warlord Hongi Hika, who accepted 48 felling axes for the land and also offered Marsden and his staff protection from invading tribes.

Overlooking both buildings is the more ancient **Kororipo Pa**, which served as chief Hongi Hika's more basic domain (until, not surprisingly, he had a European-style house built nearby in the 1820s).

The Kerikeri Basin offers a number of pleasant short walks along the river, the most notable of which takes in the 27-m **Rainbow Falls**. You can also take a one-hour heritage steamboat cruise aboard the **SS Eliza Hobson** ① *T09-407 9229 steamship.co.nz, Sun-Fri 1400, $35, under-12s half price, under 5s free, book in advance*.

As well as its fruit, Kerikeri is also famous for its arts and crafts. Ask for the free leaflet **Kerikeri Art and Craft Trail** ① *at the Kerikeri visitor centre, Cobham Rd, T09-4079297, kerikeri. co.nz, Mon-Fri 0900-1700, Sat 1000-1200*.

North to the Cape

Provided you have your own transport, the roads that branch off SH1 to the coast north of Kerikeri offer stunning coastal scenery and some secluded beaches that are well worth visiting. About 15 km north of Kerikeri the road loops to the coast taking in settlements and hideaways including Matauri Bay where you can soak up some views of the Cavalli islands and pay homage to the Greenpeace vessel *Rainbow Warrior* that was laid to rest just offshore in 1987 after it was sunk by terrorists in Auckland in 1985 (see box, opposite). A small memorial sits on the hill overlooking the islands.

Rejoining SH1 again near Whangaroa you then meet the sweeping shores of Doubtless Bay with its mainly retirement communities of Mangonui, Coopers Beach and Cable Bay, before cutting across the picturesque Karikari Peninsula on your way to the last significant northern outpost and predominantly Maori enclave of Kaitaia.

Kaitaia and the Aupouri Peninsula

The Aupouri Peninsula forms the northernmost tip of New Zealand and satisfies that strange human desire to reach the very end of everything. Like some long sandy pier, people naturally gravitate and rush as if late for an appointment for an obligatory photo with the lighthouse and a signpost to famous cities with distances that bend the mind. And to further satisfy that sense of 'what now?' an organized trip is made truly memorable with a blast down Ninety Mile Beach on the peninsula's western flank. It is, in fact, less than 90 miles and nearer to 90 km. Clearly, whoever first measured it was northbound and in a bit of a rush.

The Rainbow Warrior

Matauri Bay has always been a popular holiday spot, but assumed additional national fame when the wreck of the Greenpeace vessel *Rainbow Warrior* was laid to rest off the Cavallis in 1987. The famous flagship was bombed by French secret service through an act of terrorism in Auckland in 1985. The idea was to prevent her leading a protest flotilla to the French nuclear test grounds on the Pacific atoll of Mururoa. Her sunken hull, 3 km offshore, provides a home to countless sea creatures while an impressive memorial on the hill overlooking the islands near the beach pays tribute to the ship, her crew (one of which was killed) and the continuing cause for a nuclear-free region. The incident sparked an international outcry and New Zealanders are in no hurry to forget, or forgive. There is an echo of Maori history, spirit and support in the bay with the waka (war canoe) *Mataatua II* located near the campground. The history of this legendary canoe led to the local tribe, the Ngati Kura, offering the remains and the mana (spirit) of the modern day *Rainbow Warrior* a final resting place. The wreck is now a popular diving spot.

Kaitaia at the base of the peninsula is the main rural service centre for the Far North. It is predominantly Maori with a smattering of Dalmatian blood – mainly Croats who came during the kauri gum boom years of the late 1800s. For the tourist it provides a gateway to Cape Reinga and you can join the various coach trips north from here.

With your own wheels it will take about 1½ hours to reach the cape from Kaitaia. The road is sealed all the way, but watch your speed – many a budding Lewis Hamilton in their Maui campervan has come to grief along this stretch. Although Ninety Mile Beach is classified as a highway, you are not advised to take anything other than a 4WD vehicle onto the sand. For those in rental cars (which are not insured on the sand) who cannot resist the temptation to do so, be warned: it will probably all end in tears. If you are short of time the best way to see the peninsula is to join the many coach tours from Paihia, Mangonui or Kaitaia.

For most visitors, sadly, the visit to this amazing area will be all too brief and revolve around Cape Reinga and the lighthouse. The views from the hill above the lighthouse are stunning and in stormy weather you can see the Tasman Sea and Pacific in an uneasy union, and as far as the Three Kings Islands, 57 km offshore. The northland coastline has claimed over 140 vessels and many lives since 1808, with the majority falling foul around the cape. The lighthouse was built in 1941 and contains the lens from the original lighthouse built on Motuopao Island to the south. Beside the lighthouse is the obligatory multi-destination signpost for that vital digital memento. Hello Mum!

The Hokianga and Kauri Coast

From Ahipara (west of Kaitaia) the road turns south via Herekino to Narrows Landing on the Hokianga Harbour. There you meet the ferry to **Rawene** ① *T09-405 2602, daily 0730-1930, light vehicles $15, foot/car passengers $3*, and the heart of Hokianga.

There is little to hold the visitor in Rawene except the laid-back **Boatshed Café and Gallery** ① *T09-405 7728*, and the historic 1868 Clendon House the former residence of James Clendon, a local dignitary.

To the east of Rawene and 14 km north of the small settlement Taheke (off SH12) is one of Northland's newest natural tourist attractions, though at almost three million years

ld, new is hardly an apt description. The **Wairere Boulders** ⓘ *McDonnell Rd, Horeke, T09-*
?01 9935, wairereboulders.co.nz, daily, $10, child $5, can loosely be described as a valley
of ancient basalt rocks formed by ancient pyroclastic flows that have since eroded and
become stacked upon one another, creating a strange geological labyrinth, or stream of
rocks. Allow three hours.

Opononi and Omapere

Back in Rawene you join the SH12 to Opononi and Omapere and all points south to
Dargaville. These two converging waterfront villages are the main resorts in the Hokianga.
The villages and the harbour entrance are dominated by the impressive bare sand dunes
that grace its northern shore. They rise to a height of 100 m and at sunset glow with an
orange radiance. It was here in the Hokianga Harbour, in the 10th century, that the great
Polynesian explorer Kupe is said to have first set foot in Aotearoa (New Zealand) from
his homeland of Hawaiki. Other than that, both Opononi and Omapere were somewhat
insignificant until the appearance of a solitary wild dolphin in 1955. Opo, as she was
christened, won the hearts of the nation and subsequently put little Opononi on the map.
Most activity in Opononi and Omapere revolves around the two hotels, particularly the
Omapere Tourist Hotel with its deck over looking the harbour.

The small **Omapere Museum** ⓘ *0930-1630, free*, housed above the information centre,
has some interesting historical stories, pictures and items, of which the original and highly
entertaining 'Tally Ho' video about Opo the dolphin stands out. There are some fine coastal
walks in the area and the **i-SITE** ⓘ *T09-405 8869*, can advise.

The Waipoua Forest

Just south of Omapere you bid farewell to the coast and the Hokianga and enter kauri
country. Waipoua, Mataraua and Waima forests make up the largest remaining tract of
native forest in Northland, and the Waipoua and Trounson kauri forests contain 300 species
of tree including the great kauri with two of the finest examples and living monuments
to these magnificent and awe-inspiring trees. The Waipoua Forest is home to the largest
remaining individuals, including the much-loved and ancient **Tane Mahuta** or 'Lord of the
Forest'. For lovers of life and for those who have a healthy respect for nature, to visit this
great tree is something of a pilgrimage. For those who have never really thought about it,
it is a fine place to start. Look for the signs and car parks. The **Waipoua Forest visitor centre**
ⓘ *DoC, off SH12 towards the southern end of the park, T09-4393011, doc.govt.nz, daily 0900-*
1700, contains a museum and provides information.

About 30 km south of Waipoua and 10 km towards the coast is the aquatic summer
playground of the **Kai Iwi Lakes**. This is a favourite Northland holiday spot for those
wanting to enjoy the combination of endless beach and surf, together with the more
sedate inland waters of the three main lakes.

Dargaville and Kaipara Harbour

Just south of the lakes is **Dargaville**, once a bustling port and the largest town on the west
coast of Northland. It straddles the banks of the Wairoa River, a tributary of the mighty
Kaipara Harbour. With a combined coastline of over 3200 km, the Kaipara is one of the
largest natural harbours in the world. Irish timber merchant Joseph Dargaville founded
the town in 1872, when the district was already the enclave of a large group of Dalmatian
settlers. Kauri timber was the name of the game and for many years and it was an important
export centre. Today it serves as the main centre for the farms with their barren fields on

which the great kauri once stood, and the river transports very little except ducks. The region as a whole is also known as the kumara capital of the country producing the best of this sweet potato introduced by the early Polynesian navigators. The main attraction in the region – and one of the best in Northland – is the **Kauri Museum** ① *Church Rd, T09 431 7417, kauri-museum.com, daily 0900-1700, $25, child $8*, near the village of Matakohe 45 km south of Dargaville. The museum houses a number of imaginative displays that offer a detailed insight into the natural history of the kauri and man's exploitation and love affair with the great tree.

From Matakohe the SH12 meets the main SH1 at Brynderwyn (26 km). From there it is a 114-km journey south to Auckland.

Northland listings

For hotel and restaurant price codes and other relevant information, see pages 9-14.

🛏 Where to stay

Whangarei *p41, maps p41 and p42*
$$$-$ Whangarei Top Ten Holiday Park, 24 Mair St, T09-437 6856, whangareitop10.co.nz. This motor park has the best facilities and is the most convenient in Whangarei.
$$ Tide Song, Taiharuru Estuary, Beasley Rd, Onerahi, T09-436 1959, tidesong.co.nz. Excellent, peaceful B&B offering a self-contained 2-bedroom loft and a double en suite in a bush and seaside setting 30 mins east of Whangarei.

Paihia *p44, map p45*
$$$-$ Haruru Falls Resort Panorama (and motor park), Old Wharf Rd, 6 km northwest of Paihia, T0800-757525, harurufalls.co.nz. Standard apartment, hotel rooms and motel units, powered sites, pool, restaurant and bar all within view of the Haruru Falls. Courtesy shuttle to Paihia.
$$ Allegra House, 39 Bayview Rd, T09-402 7932, allegra.co.nz. Conveniently located in the heart of Paihia with fine views across the bay to Russell and beyond, this modern home offers the choice of conventional B&B accommodation or a spacious self-contained apartment with an extra en suite if required. There are 2 B&B rooms that can accommodate single, twin or double. Both

have TV, tea and coffee-making facilities and a fridge. Owners are fluent in both German and French. Internet and off-street parking. Minimum 2-night stay.

Russell *p46*
$$$ The Duke of Marlborough, Waterfront, Russell, T09-403 7829, theduke.co.nz. Right on the waterfront and oozing all the gracious charm its 150-year location deserves, 'The Duke', as it is affectionately known, offers some welcome relief from the tourist hype of Paihia. The refurbished modern rooms perhaps deflect from the establishment's historic charm, but there is no denying the quality, with some affording fine bay views and a large bath or spa. The cosy bar and à la carte restaurant offers a fine place to relax. When you're here, it's difficult to believe, the village was once called the Hell Hole of the Pacific. Continental breakfast included, cooked breakfast extra.
$$$-$$ Arcadia Lodge, 10 Florence Av, Matauwhi Bay, T09-403 7756, arcadialodge.co.nz. Lovingly restored, historic Tudor house with 3 characterful, spacious suites, great breakfast.

North to the Cape *p47*
$$$$ Kauri Cliffs Lodge, Matauri Bay, T09-407 0010, kauricliffs.com. One of the top 100 lodges in the world set on 2500 ha near Matauri Bay, Northland. Superb luxury facilities, memorable views and an

international standard golf course. Tariffs also remain within the realistic as opposed to the ridiculous. If you really want to spoil yourself in Northland and can swing a golf club then this is the venue.

$$ Carneval Ocean View B&B, 360 SH10, Cable Bay, T09-406 1012, carneval.co.nz. Perched on a hill overlooking Doubtless Bay this modern B&B provides a fine base from which to explore the Aupouri Peninsula. Fresh en suites with contemporary decor offering either garden or ocean views. Organized trips to Cape Reinga and a range of other aquatic based activities can be arranged.

$$-$ Matauri Bay Holiday Park, Matauri Bay (30 km north of Kerikeri), T09-405 0525. Tight on the beach near the Rainbow Warrior memorial hill, which sadly affects the view, but a great spot nonetheless. Powered sites, self-contained chalets and general store. Dive trips a speciality.

Kaitaia and the Aupouri Peninsula p47
Motor parks
$$-$ Waitiki Landing, SH1, 20 km south of the Cape, T09-409 7508. Cheap powered tent sites, bunks and en suite cabins. Camp kitchen. Restaurant on site.
$$-$ YHA Ahipara Motor Camp and Backpackers, 168 Takahe St, Ahipara (14 km southwest of Kaitia), T09-409 4864, ahiparamotorcamp.co.nz. Good option for campervans, tents, backpackers or self-contained cabins. Camp kitchen.

The Hokianga amd Kauri Coast p48
$$ Copthorne Hotel and Motel, SH12, Omapere, T09-405 8737, omapere.co.nz. A fine spot next to the beach and the wharf. Modern hotel rooms with kitchenette, TV and internet. Pool, restaurant and bar.

Motor parks
$$$-$ Kauri Coast Top Ten Holiday Park, Trounson Park Rd, Kaihu (30 km north of Dargaville), T09-439 0621, kauricoasttop10.

co.nz. Best motor park between Opononi and Dargaville. Powered sites and cabins in a site next to the river. Clean and modern. Guided night tours to Trounson Kauri Reserve in summer to hear kiwi, see glow-worms and native eels, $20.

🍴 Restaurants

Auckland to the Bay of Islands p40, maps p41 and p42
$$$ Kamakura Restaurant, 29 The Strand, Russell, T09-403 7771, kamakura.co.nz. Mon-Sun 0600-late. Waterfront dining at arguably the Bay of Island's best restaurant. Pacific Rim with Asian influences. Book a window table and watch the sunset.
$$$-$$ A Deco, 70 Kamo Rd, Whangarei, T09-459 4957. Lunch Wed-Fri, dinner Tue-Sat. As the name suggests, an art deco property housing an award-winning restaurant. Imaginative and beautifully presented Pacific Rim cuisine.
$$$-$$ Salt Brasserie, 78-94 Marsden Rd, Paihia, T09-402 6199. One of the more reliable options in Paihia offering Pacific Rim, Asian and Classic European-style cuisines. Situated overlooking the lonesome Motumaire Island. Try the seafood tasting platter as a starter.
$$-$ Bob Café, 29 Bank St, Whangarei, T09-4380881. Mon-Fri 0800-1800, Sat 0730-1500, Sun 0900-1500. Convenient and quality coffee or lunch stop while heading through town. Licensed.
$$-$ Waikokopu Café, Waitangi National Reserve, T09-4026275. Daily 0900-1700. Undoubtedly one of the best places for daytime eating in and around Paihia with pleasant surroundings and a highly imaginative menu including the sumptuous 'Whalers Breakfast'. BYO and licensed.

North to the Cape p47
$$$-$ Carrington Club Restaurant and Karikari Estate Café, Maitai Bay Rd, T09-4087222, heritagehotels.co.nz/Carrington-Resort. Lunch and dinner. Bookings advised.

It is a bit of a drive to this 5-star golf/vineyard resort on the Karikari Peninsula, but the food, wine and scenery are worth it. Fresh local seafood a speciality complimented by award-winning wines from the winery. For lighter meals during the day you may also consider the Karikari Estate Cafe.

$$-$ Mangonui Fish and Chip Shop, Beach Rd, Mangonui, T09-4060478. Open 0800-2100. A northland institution set waterside just north of the village and a popular stopping point for those on day trips to the cape.

⊙ What to do

Tutukaka Coast *p41*
Diving
Dive Tutukaka, T09-434 3867, diving.co.nz. The main dive company for the Poor Knights Islands, internationally recognized dive sites. Offer dive courses, snorkeling, kayak, and whale- and dolphin-watching activities. Full dive day (2 dives) from $225.

The Bay of Islands *p44, map p45*
Golf
Waitangi Golf Club, T09-402 7713, waitangigolf.co.nz. An excellent 18-hole course.

Tour operators
The minute you arrive in Paihia you are under pressure to book, book, book and buy, buy, buy. There is a huge range of water-based tour and activity options. Most of the day excursions options to Cape Reinga are also booked from here. The best thing to do is to take your time and to take advice from the unbiased VIC before venturing into the booking mall on the waterfront. The main player is **Fullers Great Sights**: T09-402 7421, T0800-653339, dolphincruises.co.nz, which offer tours around the islands with Cape Brett's famous Hole in the Rock being

the main highlight. Trips generally involve combinations of activities from simple sightseeing to island stops, lunch cruises and swimming with dolphins. **Coastal Kayakers**: T09-402 8105, coastal kayakers. co.nz, offers half- or full-day guided trips (some up river to Haruru Falls) and also the excellent 3-day experience. 3 days on a remote bay with a kayak to explore the islands can be a great adventure, and is a chance to encounter dolphins.

Walking
Cape Brett Walk, one of the finest walks in Northland following the ridge of Cape Brett to the lighthouse and DoC Cape Brett Hut. With a clear view across the Bay of Islands, it provides some spectacular coastal scenery. It will take an entire day (about 8 hrs) to walk the 20 km to the hut though if you cannot face the return journey, book a water taxi back to Rawhiti from just below the hut with T0800 387 892, islandshuttle. co.nz. To attempt the walk and stay in the hut you must first pay a hut fee of $10 and a track fee of $30 at the DoC visitor centre in Russell, T09-403 9005. For organized trips contact Cape Brett Walkways, T09-403 8823, capebrettwalks.co.nz.

North to the Cape *p47*
Golf
Kauri Cliffs Golf Course, Kauri Cliffs, Matauri Bay Rd, T09-405 1900, kauricliffs.com. One of the most scenic golf courses in the country, but expensive at over $200 a round.

⊖ Transport

Northland *p39*
All the main centres in Northland are served by bus and i-SITES can assist with bookings. There are no rail services.

See also Visiting Warkworth and the Kowhai Coast, page 40.

Coromandel Peninsula

The Coromandel Peninsula offers varied and spectacular coastal scenery, rugged mountain bush and a relaxed lifestyle that has, during the summer holidays, drawn Aucklanders south for decades.

The west coast, bounded by the Firth of Thames, is the most undeveloped side of the peninsula. It has a ragged coastline of islands and pebble beaches, lined with some of the best examples of pohutukawa trees in the country. For three weeks in December, with their olive evergreen leaves that crown the gnarled trunks, they flower in a radiant mantle of crimson, earning them the label of New Zealand's Christmas tree.

In contrast, the east coast is a plenitude of beautiful bays and sandy beaches, with Cathedral Cove and New Chums Beach being two of the most celebrated in the North Island. Here you will find most of the population, from the transitory tourist in the holiday townships of Whitianga and Whangamata to the rich retiree in the rather sterile resorts of Matarangi and Pauanui.

Between the two coasts a dominating backbone of bush-clad mountains make up the Coromandel Forest Park, with its wealth of walks and historic logging and mining remains. In summary, if you have the time, put the Coromandel firmly on the travelling agenda.

Coromandel West Coast

Visiting Coromandel West Coast

Tourist information Thames i-SITE visitor centre ① *206 Pollen St, Thames, T07-868 7284, thamesinfo.co.nz.* **Coromandel i-SITE visitor centre** ① *355 Kapanga Rd, Coromandel, T07 866 8598, coromandeltown.co.nz.* **Whitianga i-SITE visitor centre** ① *55 Albert St, Whitianga, T07-866 5555, whitianga.co.nz.*

Thames

① *T07-868 8514, goldmine-experience.co.nz. Daily 1000-1600, $15, child $5, includes tour underground.*

The town of Thames is at the western base of the Coromandel Peninsula at the mouth of the Waihou River and fringe of the Hauraki Plains. Behind the town rise the bush-clad hills of the Coromandel Forest Park. Thames serves as the gateway to the peninsula, either north to Coromandel town and the west coast, or across the heart of the forest park to Tairua and the east coast. It is the largest town on the Coromandel and was one of the largest towns in New Zealand during the peak of the kauri logging and gold mining era of the late 1800s, though you would not guess it now. Other than essential services there is little in the town to hold the tourist back, except perhaps a few historic buildings and the old Gold Mine and Stamper Battery.

Coromandel Forest Park

① *T07-867 9080, doc.govt.nz.*

The Kauaeranga Valley is the main access point to the Coromandel Forest Park. The forest was, in the late 1800s, one of the most extensive kauri logging areas in the North Island. At the head of the valley (13 km east of Thames) there is a DoC visitor centre, from where you can plan numerous short, day or multi-day walks taking in mining relics.

The coast road from Thames to Coromandel Town is scenic but very windy and quite dangerous so take your time. On the way, the **Rapaura Watergardens** ① *6 km up the Tapu–Coroglen Rd, T07-868 4821, rapaurawatergardens.co.nz, 0900-1700, $12, child $6,* are worth a look, with lots of lily ponds. It also has a café and self-catering lodge ($275), or cottage ($165) accommodation.

Coromandel Township

① *T07-866 8703, drivingcreekrailway.co.nz. Trains run daily at 1015, 1400, also 1130, 1245, 1515 and 1630 in summer, $25, child $10, family $60.*

Coromandel Township has a wonderful bohemian village feel and a warm atmosphere. The locals, many of whom are artists, are friendly and contented souls who walk about with a knowing smile, as if they are well aware they have come to the right place. Again, gold and kauri in the late 1800s were the attraction, and some old buildings remain, though sadly not the beautiful native bush that once cloaked the hills. Just north of the town one of New Zealand's most famous potters, Barry Brickell, has created – along with many fine works from his kiln – a quirky **Driving Creek Railway**. It is a delight and a construction of budget engineering genius, together with artistic creativity and environmental sensitivity.

The 309 to Whiti

ⓘ T07-866 7191, waiauwaterworks.co.nz. Daily 0900-1700, closed in winter, $20, child $15.
The old 309 road, which starts just south of Coromandel Town, winds its way 22 km to Whitianga and has a number of attractions along the way. The first stop on the 309, 4.5 km from Coromandel, is the charming **Waiau Waterworks**, which is a garden full of fascinating whimsical water sculptures and gadgets. This is Kiwi ingenuity and imagination at its wonderfully eccentric best.

A short distance up the road from the waterworks there is a track on the left that takes you a further 2 km to the start of the Castle Rock Walk (standard cars will be fine, walk one to two hours return). The aptly named **Castle Rock** (490 m) is a particularly knobbly-looking volcanic plug that commands a wonderful view of the northern end of the peninsula.

Just over 7 km up the 309 are the **Waiau Falls** (15-minute walk). Less than 1 km further is the Kauri Grove, a stand of ancient kauri (20-minute walk). From here you can return to Coromandel Town or carry on to Whitianga.

North to Colville and the Cape

North of Coromandel Town, the Colville Road rejoins the coast at Papa Aroha (Land of Love) and Amodeo Bay. From these charming bays you will be able to feast your eyes on Mount Moehau, which at 893 m is the highest mountain in the north of the North Island. The summit is sacred to Maori and tapu (out of bounds) but you can access it in part along a very pleasant riverside walk at Te Hope Stream.

Note also the wonderfully old and gnarled **pohutukawa trees** that grace the shoreline in this area. These are some of the best examples in the country, and in December flower in a gorgeous crimson mantle. From this point you are entering perhaps the most remote and scenic area of the Coromandel Peninsula with an atmosphere all of its own. The beach at **Waitete Bay**, 5 km north of Amodeo Bay, is a cracker and a favourite haunt in summer. From here the road climbs over the hill and falls again to the historic settlement of Colville, with its amazingly well-stocked **general store** ⓘ T07-8666805, Mon-Thu 0830-1700, Fri 0830-1730, Sat/Sun 0830-1700. Next door, the Colville Café is a great place for lunch.

North of Colville you can continue to the cape along the Port Jackson Road. After negotiating numerous idyllic pebble bays, the road eventually climbs round the northern tip of the cape and falls steeply to **Port Jackson** and Fletcher Bay where the road ends. From here you can enjoy great views of Great Barrier Island, seemingly only a stone's throw away across the Colville Channel.

Coromandel East Coast

Coromandel Town to Whitianga

From Coromandel Town the SH25 winds its way east, over the ranges, offering fine views, before descending steeply to Te Rerenga and Whangapoua Harbour. Whangapoua village, 4 km north of the junction at Te Rerenga, is essentially made up of holiday homes and beaches that come alive in the summer months. A 30-minute walk north from the road end in Whangapoua is **New Chums Beach**, which is one of the best beaches in the Coromandel. The fact that you cannot drive there and have to negotiate the headland by foot seems to protect its beauty. Even in bad weather it is worth the walk. Another fine beach where you can escape the crowds is Opito Bay, accessed via Kuaotunu 17 km north of Whitianga.

Whitianga

Whitianga is a very popular holiday town on the shores of beautiful Mercury Bay, which was given its planetary name by Captain Cook during a spot of astronomy on his brief visit in 1769. 'Whiti' (pronounced 'fitty') has much to offer, including a number of fine

1 Whitianga

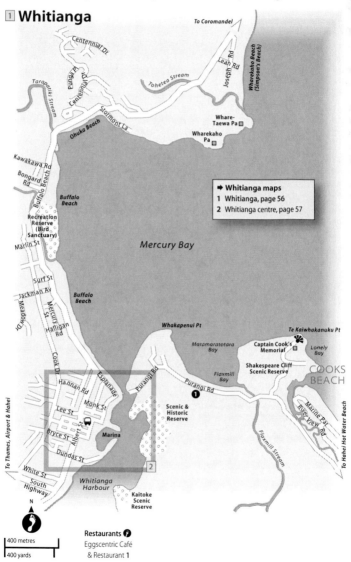

→ **Whitianga maps**
1 Whitianga, page 56
2 Whitianga centre, page 57

Mercury Bay

To Coromandel

Wharekaho Beach (Simpson's Beach)

Whare-Taewa Pa

Wharekaho Pa

Ohuka Beach

Buffalo Beach

Recreation Reserve (Bird Sanctuary)

Buffalo Beach

Whakapenui Pt

Maramaratotara Bay

Te Kaiwhakanuku Pt

Captain Cook's Memorial

Lonely Bay

Shakespeare Cliff Scenic Reserve

COOKS BEACH

Flaxmill Bay

Purangi Rd

Scenic & Historic Reserve

Marina

Whitianga Harbour

Kaitoke Scenic Reserve

To Thames, Airport & Hahei

To Hahei Hot Water Beach

N

400 metres
400 yards

Restaurants
Eggscentric Café & Restaurant 1

beaches within walking distance of the town. It also acts as a convenient short-cut access point, across the narrow Whitianga Harbour entrance and **Ferry Landing**, to two fine smaller resorts – Cooks Beach and Hahei. Although there is an abundance of activities to choose from, Whiti is most famous as a sea- and big-game fishing base and a trip on the water is recommended.

There are a number of short walks in the area and the i-SITE can advise. The **Shakespeare Cliff Scenic Reserve** accessed via the ferry and Ferry Landing is recommended for its great bay views.

Whiti also has a couple of excellent **bone carving** studios (see page 60), which offer the opportunity to carve your own bone pendant – traditionally from whale bone but now typically from beef bone.

Hahei, Cathedral Cove and Hot Water Beach

Hahei is a wonderful little unspoiled coastal settlement, 35 km by road from Whitianga. A shorter route is via the ferry from Whitianga. Both Hahei and Cooks Beach have wonderful beaches especially Hahei Beach as it looks over a wealth of islands and rock outcrops. But the real jewel in the region's crown, indeed perhaps for the whole peninsula, is the amazing Cathedral Cove, which guards the Te Whanganui-A-Hei Marine Reserve. Access is by boat or a half-hour walk. The track starts from a glorious lookout point just north of Hahei on Grange Road.

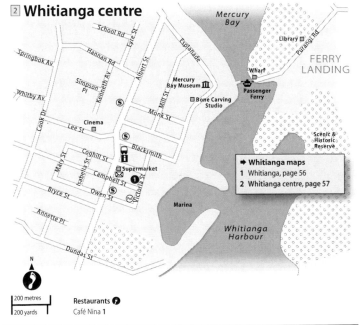

② **Whitianga centre**

➡ **Whitianga maps**
1 Whitianga, page 56
2 Whitianga centre, page 57

Restaurants ❼
Café Nina 1

About 15 km south of Hahei is Hot Water Beach where you can dig a hole in the sand t access natural hot water. You can only do this for about two hours each side of low tide. N spade? The Hot Water Beach Store hires them out for a small fee.

Opoutere and Whangamata

Opoutere is one of the Coromandel's best-kept secrets. It has a quiet and magical atmosphere with sweeping white-sand Ocean Beach, guarded by the Wharekawa Harbou and a narrow tract of forest. At the tip of the sand spit is the Wharekawa Wildlife Refug where oystercatchers and rare New Zealand dotterel breed in summer. The beach can b accessed from the car park around the corner from the Opoutere Youth Hostel (YHA).

Just south of Oputere is the town of Whangamata, which is the main surfing venue on the Coromandel. The often-busy beach is over 4 km long, but a far quieter option i Whiritoa Beach and lagoon, 12 km south. It also offers a lovely bush walk, heading north Whangamata is also a base for trips to the outer islands, including Mayor Island.

Waihi

Waihi was once host to 1200 mines producing half of the country's gold and earning i the reputation as the most famous mining town in New Zealand. Between 1878 and 1952 the town produced over 174,000 kg of gold and 1 million kg of silver. Today the mos impressive evidence of the town's mining history is the enormous open-pit **Martha Mine** which sits like a huge, but strangely discrete bomb crater right in the centre of town. From a lookout behind the **Waihi VIC** ① *Upper Seddon St, T07-863 6715, waihi.org.nz, daily 0900-1700*, you can watch huge earth-moving trucks relentlessly winding their way in and out of the massive terraced hole.

Given the town's 'rich' history the **Waihi Arts Centre and Museum** ① *54 Kenny St, T07-863 8386, waihi.co.nz/arts/museum, Mon-Fri 1000-1600, Sat-Sun 1330-1600, $5, child $3*, is well worth a look. It displays an array of mining memorabilia and interesting working models, including a miniature stamping battery. Inevitably you leave a lot wiser about the incredible 175-km-long network of tunnels that insidiously lies beneath your feet.

Nearby, the Ohinemuri River winds its dramatic way west, through the **Karangahake Gorge**, where there are a number of interesting walks and mining relics (DoC leaflet available from the VIC). A vintage steam train, the **Goldfields Railway** ① *T07-863 9020, waihirail.co.nz, trains leave from Wrigley St, daily at 1000, 1145, 1345, $15 return, child $8; café at Waikino station, daily 1000-1600*, runs 6.5 km and 30 minutes into the gorge from Waihi to Waikino.

If you want to go to the beach, head for the popular surfers' hangout at **Waihi Beach**, 11 km to the east. A pleasant 45-minute coastal walk at the northern end of the beach will take you to the very pretty Orokawa Bay.

Coromandel Peninsula listings

For hotel and restaurant price codes and other relevant information, see pages 9-14.

🛏 Where to stay

West Coast *p54*

$$$-$$ Pottery Lane Cottages, 15 Pottery Lane, Coromandel, T07-866 7171, potterylncottage@xtra.co.nz. 2 good-value, self-contained cottages in a garden setting and within a short stroll from the village centre. The first has a separate double and twin room while the second is smaller and open plan. Both have character and are tastefully decorated. There is also a loft room with kitchenette. Off street parking.

Motor parks

$$$-$ Miranda Holiday Park, Front Miranda Rd (30 km west of Thames), T07-867 3205, mirandaholidaypark.co.nz. Although some distance before Thames this is an excellent motor park with above-average facilities, plus its own hot pool. Will get your visit to the Coromandel off to a good start.

$$-$ Coromandel Holiday Park, 636 Rings Rd, Coromandel, T07-866 8830. Centrally located with good facilities and modern cabins.

East Coast *p55*

$$ The Church, 87 Beach Rd, Hahei, T07-866 3533, thechurchhahei.co.nz. The accommodation takes the form of attached wooden studio units, separate studio or self-contained cottages surrounding a church (restaurant) and surrounded by private gardens. 2 of the self-contained cottages have an open fire adding to the cosy ambience.

$$-$ Opoutere Youth Hostel (YHA), 389 Opoutere Rd, Opoutere, T07-865 9072. A fine peaceful place to stay with great facilities, short walks nearby, and a lovely view across the harbour.

Motor parks

$$$-$ Hahei Holiday Resort (motor park), Harsant Av, Hahei, T07-866 3889, haheiholidays.co.nz. Right on the beach is this fine and spacious facility with self-contained (beachfront) lodges and backpacker accommodation. Camp kitchen.

$$-$ Mill Creek Bird and Campervan Park, 365 Mill Creek Road, Whitianga, T07-866 0166, halcyonheights.co.nz. If you love animals and/or have kids this is ideal. Peaceful and friendly with more than 400 birds of 40 species to view. Located a few kilometres south of Whitianga. Powered sites and B&B rooms with en suite.

🍴 Restaurants

West Coast *p54*

$$-$ Driving Creek Café, 180 Driving Creek Rd, Coromandel Town, T07-866 7066. Daily 0900-1700. Independent and not an adjunct to the railway complex. Laid-back, arty café largely demonstrative of the township itself. Good coffee, home baking and organic cuisine. Internet.

$$-$ Peppertree Restaurant and Bar, Coromandel Town, T07-866 8211. Daily from 0900. Reliable fine dining option in Coromandel with a lunch and mainly seafood dinner menu. It has a pleasant interior, bar and outdoor eating area. On summer evenings book in advance.

East Coast *p55*

$$-$ Café Nina, Behind the i-SITE visitor centre at 20 Victoria St, Whitianga, T07-866 5440. Daily from 0800 and 1730 for dinner. The finest café in town. Small and bustling, it covers a range of healthy and imaginative dishes.

$$-$ Eggsentric Café and Restaurant, Purangi Rd, Flaxmill Bay (1 km east of Ferry Landing), Whitianga T07-866 0307, eggsentriccafe.co.nz. Tue-Fri 1000-late, Sat/Sun 0900-late. Without doubt the most colourful place around and at times the liveliest, whose artistic and multi-talented owners put on organized and often impromptu musical performances and poetry readings. Licensed and BYO.

$$ The Church, 87 Beach Rd, Hahei, T07-866 3797, thechurchhahei.co.nz. Closed Sun/Mon. One of the region's most popular restaurants set in a restored turn-of-the-20th-century church.

O Shopping

West Coast *p54*
Moko Art Gallery, 24 Pye Pl, Hot Water Beach, just opposite the main car park, Coromandel, T07-866 3367, moko.co.nz. The arts and crafts are top class, reasonably priced and very Kiwi.

O What to do

East Coast *p55*
Bone carving
Bay Carving, next to the museum on the Esplanade, Whitianga, T07-866 4021, dreamland.co.nz/baycarving. Open 0900-1600, evenings by appointment. A very well equipped bone-carving studio and provides expert tuition (2-3 hrs from $40-80).

Kayaking
Cathedral Cove Sea Kayaking, Hahei, T07-866 3877, seakayaktours.co.nz. Offers kayak hire and half- or full-day kayak trips from $85 with all equipment provided. Courtesy transport to/from Whitianga Ferry.

Tours
Cave Cruzer, T0800-427893, T02-586 6744, cavecruzer.co.nz. A rigid inflatable that can take you on a range of tours around the bay from 1-3 hrs ($40-90), taking in the main coastal sights including Cathedral Cove.
Hahei Explorer Tours, Hahei Beach, T07-866 3910, glassbottomboatwhitianga. co.nz/haheiexplorer. If you want to experience Cathedral Cove from the water, this is an excellent trip. Daily scenic trips on board a nippy inflatable cost $65, child $40, for 2 hrs. The tour also takes in caves and a blowhole not accessible by foot.

O Transport

Coromandel Peninsula *p53, maps p56 and p57*
All the main centres on the Coromandel Peninsula are served by bus and i-SITES can assist with bookings. There are no rail services.

Intercity offers coach services to and from the Coromandel. The i-SITE visitor centre in Thames or Whitianga act as agents. A number of bus tour companies offer shuttle, personalized or specialist tour options, including: **Go Kiwi Shuttles**, T07-866 0336, go-kiwi.co.nz, Auckland to Thames from $27, Whitianga from $36, shuttle plus tours and charter; and **Coromandel Explorer Tours**, T07-866 3506, coromandeltours.co.nz, day tour from $250, 2-day from $420 (plus accommodation), 4-day tours from $820 (plus accommodation).

Contents

Footprint features

Central North Island

Rotorua and around

Of all the places in the Bay of Plenty, nature has indeed given Rotorua 'plenty'. The natural thermal wonders first attracted the Maori in the 14th century and later the Europeans, who quickly developed them in to a world-renowned tourist attraction. But nature has not always been so kind. The violent eruption of the Tarawera volcano in 1886 led to the loss of 150 lives and temporarily wiped out the tourist industry. Now, over a century later, Rotorua is deserving of its 'most visited' tourist status. The city and the region probably offer more unusual sights and activities than anywhere else in New Zealand. And although, like Taupo, it is famous for its thermal and volcanic features, lakes and fishing, the region offers a multitude of other activities. Here you can join in a Maori concert or hangi (feast), plummet over a 7-m waterfall in a raft, bike, walk and (of course) throw yourself down the infamous luge.

Arriving in Rotorua

Getting there

The i-SITE serves as the principal bus arrival and departure point. The in-house travel centre administers local and national bus, coach, air and rail ticketing, which has its own travel centre, T0800-768678.

Getting around

Baybus ① *T0800-4229287, baybus.co.nz*, is the principal local bus company, the main stop is on Pukuatua Street. Several local shuttles vie for business in providing daily transportation to the main attractions from around $25 return including **Geyserlink** ① *T0800-0004321, gyserlink.co.nz*. Contact the i-SITE for full listings.

Tourist information

Tourism Rotorua Travel and Information (i-SITE) ① *1167 Fenton St, T07-348 5179/0800-768678, rotoruanz.com, daily 0800-1800*, is one of the oldest and busiest tourist offices in the country. There is a travel centre, a currency exchange office (0800-1730), toilets, showers, a shop, and a café.

Places in Rotorua

Lake Rotorua and Ohinemutu

Lake Rotorua is the largest of the 17 lakes in the Rotorua thermal region and is, not surprisingly, a flooded volcanic crater. A feature of many of the launch trips based on the city's lakefront is the bush-clad nature reserve of Mokoia Island, scene of the classic love story of the Arawa princess Hinemoa and her suitor Tutanekai. As well as island trips the lake is a top venue for recreational activities including boating, waterskiing, flight-seeing and, above all, trout fishing.

Situated on the lakefront within the city is the former Maori settlement and thermal area of Ohinemutu. The focal point of the village is the Tamatekapua marae, a beautifully carved wharerunanga (meeting house), erected in 1939.

Just opposite the marae is the Tudor-style **St Faith's Church** ① *daily 0800-1700, free*, built in 1910. Its interior pillars, beams, rafters and pews are beautifully carved with Maori designs, and on a sandblasted window overlooking the lake a Maori Christ is portrayed, dressed in a korowai (chief's cloak). There are still boiling pools near the church that are frequently used by locals for cooking.

Government Gardens and the Rotorua Museum of Art and History

① *Queens Dr, Government Gardens, T07-350 1814, rotoruamuseum.co.nz. Daily summer 0900-2000, winter 0900-1700, $18, child $7. Guided tours hourly 1000-1600. Shop and a café.*
Fringing Lake Rotorua are the elegant Government Gardens with their well-manicured bowling greens and croquet lawns, ponds and scented roses, creating a distinctly Edwardian, colonial atmosphere. They provide the perfect setting for the Rotorua Museum of Art and History housed in the once world-famous Bath House. Built in 1908, it was designed along the lines of the European spas and attracted hundreds of clients the world over who hoped to take advantage of the thermal waters' therapeutic and curative powers. In one wing of the museum you can see some of the original baths, changing rooms and equipment, together with old photographs. Elsewhere, given the rich local Maori history,

1 Rotorua

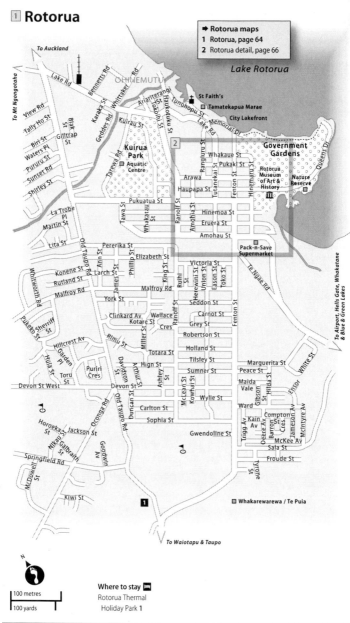

➡ **Rotorua maps**
1 Rotorua, page 64
2 Rotorua detail, page 66

Lake Rotorua

To Auckland

To Mt Ngongotaha

OHINEMUTU

St Faith's
Tamatekapua Marae
City Lakefront
Memorial Dr

Lake Rd
Bennetts Rd
Whittaket Rd
Ariariterangi St
Haukotuku St
Tunohopu St

View Rd
Tally Ho St
Biri St
Blak St
Gilltrap St
Waters Pl
Pururu St
Sunset Rd
Shirley St
Karaka St
Geddes Rd
Takaihi St
Kuirau St

Kuirau Park
Aquatic Centre
Tarewa Rd

Rangiuru St
Whakaue St
Pukaki St
Tutanekai St
Fenton St
Hinemaru St

Government Gardens
Queens Dr

Arawa
Haupapa St
Ranolf St

Rotorua Museum of Art & History 🏛
Nature Reserve

Pukuatua St

La Trobe Pl
Martin St
Tawa St
Whakaue St
Ranolf St
Amohia St
Hinemoa St
Eruera St
Amohau St

Lita St
Pererika St
Konene St
Ann St
Phillip St
Elizabeth St

Pack-n-Save Supermarket

Te Ngae Rd

To Airport, Hells Gate, Whakatane & Blue & Green Lakes

Whitworth Rd
Rutland St
Malfroy Rd
James St
Larch St
King St
Ruihi St
Victoria St
Herewini St
Union St
Eason St
Toko St
Fenton St

Pukeko St
Sheriff St
York St
Clinkard Av
Kotare Cres
Wallace Cres
Ranolf St
Seddon St
Carnot St
Grey St
Robertson St

Hillcrest Av
Garden Pl
Hula St
Toru St
Puriri Cres
Rimu St
Miller St
Totara St
High St
Holland St
Tilsley St
Sumner St

Marguerita St
Peace St
White St

Devon St West
Davidson St
Arthur St
Ashley St
Devon St
McLean St
Kowhai St
Wylie St
Ward

Maida Vale
Gibson St
Hilda St
Ensor

Horoeka St
Jackson St
Oconga Rd
Duncan St
Carlton St
Sophia St
Gwendoline St

Trigg Av
Kain Av
Barron St
Compton St
Cres
Jameson Av
McIntyre Av

Nikau St
Galbraith Av
Goodwin Av
Oeere Av
McKee Av
Sala St
Froude St

Springfield Rd
McDowell St
Kiwi St
Tyrone St

Whakarewarewa / Te Puia

To Waiotapu & Taupo

N

| 100 metres |
| 100 yards |

Where to stay 🛏
Rotorua Thermal
Holiday Park **1**

t is not surprising to find a superb collection of Te Arawa taonga (treasures) and displays that feature the great Tarawera eruption of 1886. Not to be missed is the excellent audio-visual display entitled Rotorua Stories (every 20 minutes) that has its own surprises.

Polynesian Spa

ⓘ *Lakeside, 1000 Hinemoa St, T07-348 1328, polynesianspa.co.nz. Daily 0800-2300, from $14.50, child $6.50.*

Rain or shine this is a Rotorua 'must do' and, although often very busy, it is a delight. There is a luxury spa complex and hot springs and pools, private spa pools, a family spa, shop and café. A range of massage treatments are also available. The best times to go are at lunch and dinnertime when the tour buses are elsewhere.

Te Puia (Whakarewarewa)

ⓘ *Fenton St (3 km south of the city), T07-348 9047, tepuia.com. Summer daily 0800-1800, winter 0800-100, $46, child $23, guided tours depart hourly. Maori concerts 1015, 1215, 1515, tour and concert $57.40, child $28.70. Te Po evening performance and feast, $110, child $55. General admission and Te Po $145, child $72.50. There is a shop and a café on site.*

For many, Europeans especially, this is their first exposure to thermal features and all things bubbly mud! 'Whaka' (pronounced 'Fuckka') – or brand name 'Te Puia' – now claims to be New Zealand's premier Maori cultural centre and is certainly the most commercial. The complex includes the functional Rotowhio Marae, the modern and thriving Maori Arts and Crafts Institute and of course a number of natural thermal features. The star attraction is the much-celebrated Pohutu, the country's largest geyser, and also boiling pools, silica terraces and lots of bubbling mud.

The Rotowhio Marae with its fully carved wharenui (meeting house) hosts daily cultural performances and a longer performance entitled Te Po in the evenings that includes a hangi (feast). There is a deliberate and entertaining element of interactivity with visitors. The Maori Arts and Crafts Institute was established in 1963 to ensure that the traditional artist aspects of Maori culture are not lost. A viewing platform allows visitors to see students at work in the woodcarving studio.

Waiotapu

ⓘ *Off SH5 (29 km south of Rotorua and not to be confused with Waimangu Thermal Valley 4 km before it), T07-3666333, geyserland.co.nz.Daily 0830-1700, $32.50, child $11.*

Waiotapu is, without doubt, the best thermal park in the region, with an almost surreal and colourful range of volcanic features, from mud pools and silica terraces to the famous and beautiful Champagne Pool. The full self-guided walk around the park will take about two hours and take in features with such evocative names as the Devil's Home and Thunder Crater. Without doubt, the highlight of the park is the Champagne Pool, a 62-m-deep flooded volcanic vent, the base of which boils the water to a surface temperature of around 74°C. Hot stuff.

Many time their arrival with the daily 1015 eruption of the Lady Knox Geyser, which is signposted on the Waiotapu Loop Road (off SH5). Just before the geyser, again on the Loop Road, are a number of wonderfully melodious and globulous mud pools that are separate from the park itself.

Waiotapu gets very busy. Avoid the hyperbolic daily morning show at the Lady Knox Geyser and instead head up the road to **Waikite Valley Thermal Pools** ⓘ *signposted off SH5, 4 km, T07-333 1861, hotpools.co.nz, $14*, and see the natural boiling spring. Then enjoy the hot pools while you are there.

Skyline Rotorua

ⓘ *Fairy Springs Rd, T07-347 0027, skyline.co.nz. Daily 0900-late. Gondola $25, child $12.50, gondola and 3 luge rides $41, child $31.*

Everyone who is fit and able and visits Rotorua should call in here to take a ride up the mountain in the gondolas and have a go on the infamous luge, which basically involves throwing yourself down a concrete course on a plastic tray with wheels and primitive brakes. Sounds mad? Absolutely! Other more conventional activity options include helicopter trips, mountain biking and then once the adrenalin has settled, there is always the scenic restaurant, with its memorable views across the city and the lake.

Hell's Gate and the Waiora Spa

ⓘ *SH30, Tikitere (15 km from Rotorua), T07-345 3151, hellsgate.co.nz. Daily 0900-2030, from $20, child $10. Park entry, mud bath and spa from $120. Massage from $100.*

Even without the very saucy looking, scantily clad couple daubing each other in mud on all the promotional material, the aptly named Hell's Gate thermal reserve and Waiora Spa

② Rotorua detail

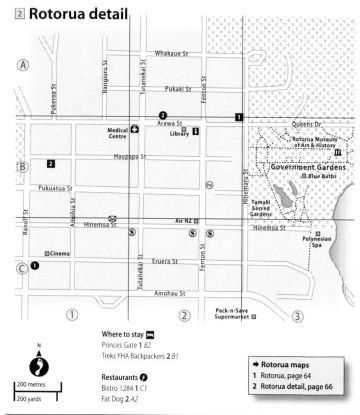

Where to stay 🛏
Princes Gate **1** *B2*
Treks YHA Backpackers **2** *B1*

Restaurants 🍴
Bistro 1284 **1** *C1*
Fat Dog **2** *A2*

➡ **Rotorua maps**
1 Rotorua, page 64
2 Rotorua detail, page 66

200 metres
200 yards

is a thoroughly steamy affair. The 10 ha of thermal features are set on two levels separated by a tract of bush. With all that mineral rich bubbly mud about it would seem rude not to create a mud spa and there are a number of attractive options from massage or sulphur spas, to the wonderfully messy and therapeutic mud facials, scrubs and (best of all) private mud baths. Who could resist?

Rainbow Springs Kiwi Wildlife Centre

ⅅ *Fairy Springs Rd, SH5 north (5 km), T07-350 0440, rainbowsprings.co.nz. Open 0800-2130, $35, child $22.50; prices include the Big Splash.*

The main attraction at Rainbow Springs are shoal of local trout, combined with other wildlife treats, including some very tame native birds in a free-flight aviary. The underwater viewing area is particularly popular. There is the Big Splash, a log flume ride, farm animal shows and a café on site.

Opposite the Rainbow Springs complex is the Kiwi Encounter complex. As the name suggests the attraction comes in the form of that truly enigmatic creature and national icon the kiwi, and this is undoubtedly one of the best captive-breeding displays in the country.

You will certainly see live kiwi, but that aside, the experience is only augmented by a view through to the husbandry area where you can see staff tending to incubating eggs, or, if you are very lucky, chicks (November to March).

Rotorua and around listings

For hotel and restaurant price codes and other relevant information, see pages 9-14.

⬤ Where to stay

Rotorua *p63, maps p64 and p66*
$$$ The Princes Gate, 1057 Arawa St, T07-348 1179, princesgate.co.nz. Conveniently located between the city centre and Government Gardens, the 1897 Princes Gate is a boutique hotel with plenty of character. Wide range of rooms, some fully self-contained, and replete with 4-poster beds and bath. An in-house bar/ restaurant, sauna and thermal pools all add to the appeal.
$$-$ Treks YHA Backpackers, 1278 Haupapa St, T07-349 4088, yha.co.nz. A fine modern establishment, well facilitated with a spacious kitchen and living area and tidy en suite doubles.

Motor parks
$$$-$ Rotorua Thermal Holiday Park, Old Taupo Rd, T07-346 3140, rotorua thermal.co.nz. Well-maintained, spacious and sheltered motor park with a wide

range of accommodation options from standard self- contained units to standard and en suite log cabins, powered and non-powered sites. Camp kitchen, TV lounge, small shop, licensed café and free hot pools. Also within walking distance of the Whakarewarewa (Te Puia) Thermal Reserve.
$ Waikite Valley Thermal Pools and Camp Ground, Waikite Valley Rd, Rotorua, T07-333 1861, hotpools.co.nz. A gem of a motor camp located 32 km south of Rotorua off SH5 and attached to the Waikite Thermal Pools complex. Basic but adequate facilities including powered sites, camp kitchen and free entry to pools. It is also just 7 km from the Waiotapu Thermal Reserve.

⬤ Restaurants

Rotorua *p63, maps p64 and p66*
$$$ Bistro 1284, 1284 Eruera St, T07-364 1284, bistro1284.co.nz. Tue-Sat from 1800, booking advised. A 1930s wooden townhouse with a congenial atmosphere and causing something of a stir locally having won the city's best restaurant award

4 years running. Minimalist and imaginative Pacific Rim menu with NZ venison and lamb a speciality. For entrée don't go past the roast kumara and honey soup with yoghurt and rocket.

$$ Landings Café, 537 Spencer Rd, Lake Tarawera, T07-362 8502. Daily from 0900. Book for dinner. Set on the shores of Lake Tarawera with uninterrupted views over both mountain and lake. Affordable and casual café style dining, excellent service and a cosy open fire in winter. There is also a garden bar for those lazy summer evenings.

$$-$ Fat Dog, 1161 Arawa St, T07-347 7586. Sun-Wed 0800-2100, Thu-Sat 0800-2130. Consistently rated as the best café in town, always busy and friendly with a mixed clientele. Quirky decor, local artwork, an imaginative blackboard menu and yes, the odd fat dog.

⊕ Entertainment

Rotorua *p63, maps p64 and p66*
Te Po at Te Puia (Whakarewarewa), Fenton St, T07-348 9047, tepuia.com. Te Po evening performance and feast, $110, child $55. Rotorua is arguably the best place to experience a Maori cultural performance in New Zealand, but beware; they can be horribly kitsch and commercial. One of the better experiences is the Te Po evening performance at Te Puia. It is commercial but well polished and of course there is a hangi-style meal included, as well as a tour of the famed thermal features.

⊕ What to do

Rotorua *p63, maps p64 and p66*
Aerial tours
Volcanic Air Safaris, Waterfront, T07-348 9984, T0800-800848, volcanicair.co.nz.

Has a fleet of fixed-wing and float plane aircraft as well as helicopters that take in all the local sights from $75-875.

Cycling and rafting
Kaitiaki Adventures, T07-357 2236, T0800-338736, sledge-it.com. River Sledging and rafting trips down the Kaituna River with the opportunity to learn about Maori culture on the way. Raft trip includes the highly entertaining 7-m drop of the Okere Falls, from $109.

Planet Bike, T07-346 1717, planet bike.co.nz. Offers organized trips or independent hire for the renowned Whakarewarewa Forest tracks. Try the half-day raft and bike combo trips from $160. Independent bike hire also available, from $35 for 2 hrs, $55 per day.

⊖ Transport

Rotorua *p63, maps p64 and p66*
There is a domestic **airport** at Rotorua. Rotorua is well served by south/north bound **bus services** from Auckland via Hamilton or Tauranga. The main i-SITES can assist with schedules and bookings.

See also Arriving in Rotorua, page 63.

⊕ Directory

Rotorua *p63, maps p64 and p66*
ATM ATM and currency exchange facilities at the i-SITE and all major banks are represented in the centre of the town. **Hospital** Lakes Prime Care, 1165 Tutanekai St, T07-348 1000, 0800-2200 (also 24-hr duty doctor). **Pharmacy** Central Pharmacy, 1245 Haupapa St, T07-348 6028.

Taupo and around

For those heading south from Auckland, Taupo is really the first place that begins to satisfy the imagination in terms of what New Zealand is 'supposed' to look like: wide open spaces with distant snow-capped mountains and clear blue lakes. As you come over the hill into the town on a clear day the huge expanse of Lake Taupo dwarfs the distant volcanoes of the Tongariro National Park.

Because of its position in the centre of the North Island, Taupo is the commercial headquarters for the central districts of Taupo and Ruapehu, as well as a major tourist resort. The town is very pleasant, busy and friendly, nestled close to the source of the Waikato River (the longest in the country), and lies on the northernmost bank of the huge lake, once a mighty volcanic crater. The region has a multitude of activities to enjoy. Trout fishing is the main attraction, but you can also try the more adrenalin-pumping pursuits of bungee jumping and tandem skydiving, as well as mountain biking, golf, sailing and walking.

Arriving in Taupo

Getting there
Bus station Regional buses arrive and depart from the **Travel Centre** ① *16 Gascoigne St, T07-3789032* and/or the **i-SITE Visitor Centre** ① *Tongariro St*.

Getting around
Hot Bus ① *T0508-468287, hotbus.co.nz*, is a hop-on/hop-off service that links most major attractions including the hot pools, Huka Falls and the Craters of the Moon, with an hourly service from the **i-SITE visitor centre**, 0900-1600, from $15 return.

A number of operators service the Tongariro National Park and Tongariro Crossing, daily via Turangi, including **Tongariro Expeditions** ① *T07-377 0435, thetongarirocrossing.co.nz* and **Alpine Hotbus** ① *T0508468287, alpinehotbus.co.nz*. **Taupo Taxis** ① *T07-3785100*.

Tourist information
Taupo i-SITE Visitor Centre ① *30 Tongariro St, SH1, T07-376 0027, laketauponz.co.nz, daily 0830-1700*, has all the usual information and a good range of maps. It also handles DoC enquiries and offers specialist information available on the Tongariro Crossing with up-to-date weather forecasts.

Lake Taupo

On a calm day the 619-sq-km lake – the largest in the country – can be almost mirror like, disturbed only by the wakes of boats and ducks. But it wasn't always like this. Lake Taupo is in fact the tranquil remains of one the biggest volcanic eruptions the planet has created in the last 5000 years. In AD 186 the caldera spewed out over 100 cu km of debris at up to 900 kph, covering almost the entire North Island in up to 10 m of ash. Hard to imagine. Now, however, the placid waters are famous for their copious trout and are the domain of the serious angler. The lake is also used for numerous other water-based activities including sailing, cruising, windsurfing and waterskiing. The i-SITE visitor centre can provide the numerous operator listings including local fishing charters and guides.

Most of the longer cruises take in the **Maori rock carvings** which is essentially a huge face complete with moko (tattoos) that can only be seen from the water and adorn an entire rock face in Mine Bay, 8 km southwest across the lake. Although impressive, they were only created in recent years, which does dampen the excitement.

Just west of the town centre the **Waikato River** (the longest in the country) begins its 425-km journey to the Tasman Sea and winds its merry way north behind the town and towards the **Huka Falls** and **Wairakei Park**.

Hot pools

The **AC Baths** ① *at the top of Spa Rd, T07-3760350, taupovenues.co.nz/ac baths.asp, daily 0600-2100, $7, child $3*, is one of two thermal pool complexes in Taupo where you can soak away any troubles in a range of outdoor, indoor and private spa pools while the kids do their thing on the hydro-slide. The other less frenetic complex is the **Taupo DeBretts Springs Resort** ① *just off SH5, which heads west from SH1, T07-377 6502, taupodebretts. co.nz, daily 0730-2130, $20, child $10*, along the lake front at the southern edge of town. Their facilities include a massage and beauty-treatment centre.

Around Taupo

Wairakei Park

North of Taupo, Wairakei Park straddles the great Waikato River and is home to a range of attractions. Paramount is the thundering Huka Falls (signposted from the SH1, accessed via the Huka Falls Rd). Arguably the most spectacular in the North Island they are the result of the Waikato River being forced through a cleft of solid rock only 15 m wide, before falling 7 m into a cauldron of aquatic chaos and foam. Believe it or not some utter lunatics have attempted the ultimate adrenalin buzz of riding the Huka by canoe. The last time it was attempted, in 1994, two canoeists went down. One made it in about 60 seconds. The other disappeared in the torrent and reappeared minus canoe, and life, 40 minutes later.

The walking tracks that lead both north and south along the river from here are worthy of a trek on foot or mountain bike. Just up river is the exclusive retreat of Huka Lodge that frequently hosts visiting dignitaries.

Carrying along the Huka Falls Loop Road (north) you can take a small diversion to admire the view looking back at the falls, before arriving at the **Volcanic Activity Centre** ① *T07-3748375, volcanoes.co.nz, daily 1000-1700, $10, child $6*.

It's well worth a peek, if only to get an inkling of the scale and magnitude of the natural powers that lie beneath your feet. The Taupo district is in the heart of one of the most active volcanic zones in the world, the details of which are well presented in the centre.

There are models and displays, all with appropriate shaking and rumbling noises and of course close monitoring of current status.

At the roads terminus **Prawn Park** ① *T07-3748474, hukaprawnpark.co.nz, daily 0900-1530, $26, child $15*, is hailed as the world's only geothermal prawn farm, where you can join an informative tour or sample some in the Prawn Farm Restaurant.

Wairakei Park

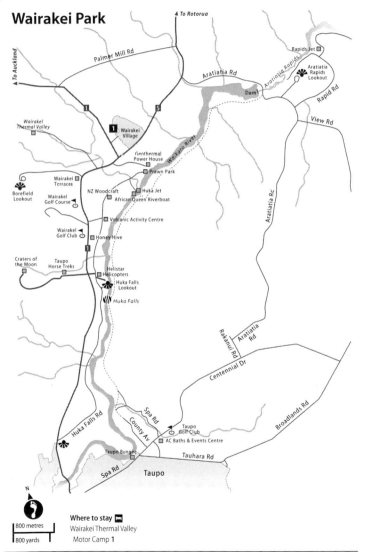

N

| 800 metres |
| 800 yards |

Where to stay 📍
Wairakei Thermal Valley
Motor Camp **1**

Alongside Prawn Park are the headquarters of **Huka Falls Jet** ① *T07-3748572 hukafallsjet.com, from $105, child $59*, offering an adrenalin-filled trip to view the base of the Huka Falls with the obligatory 360° spins. Trips depart daily every 30 minutes from 0830 to 1700 on demand.

Back on SH1 and almost directly across it, you can access the **Craters of the Moon Volcanic Reserve**. This is a very steamy affair somewhat akin to taking a stroll through a smoldering bush fire. From almost every conceivable crack and crater along the 50-minute boardwalk, steam quietly billows into the air, with only the faintest hiss giving you an indication of the forces that lie below. Friendly thermo-volunteers selling thermo souvenirs staff the reserve and the car park and they will kindly keep a hot eye on your car.

A further 7 km north is the **Wairakei Terraces** ① *T07-378 0913, wairakeiterraces.co.nz 0900-1700, $18, child $9*, which takes a historical and cultural look back in time when the Pink and White terraces, destroyed during the great Tarawera eruption of 1886, were one of the region's most famous volcanic feature. Of equal if not more interest is the **geothermal field** behind the complex where huge feeder pipes draw from the subterranean wells and form part of the region's clean green power station. There are thermal pools ($25) and therapies available.

To complete a convenient circuit back into town you can continue up SH1 and on to SH5 for about 2 km, before turning right, following the signs to Aratiatia. This will take you to a dam on the Waikato that tempers the flow of the **Aratiatia Rapids**, a similar gorge to the Huka Falls, but more jagged. The dam gates are opened at 1000, 1200 and 1400 daily in winter (plus 1600 in summer). **Rapids Jet** ① *T0800-727437, rapidsjet.com, 4 trips daily from $105, child $60*, are located at the base of the falls on Rapids Road. It's an entertaining trip beginning with a spin upstream to the base of the controlled rapids and power station, then downstream through a series of rapids with plenty of 360° spins along the way.

Orakei Korako Thermal Reserve

① *Head north from Taupo on SH1 for 27 km, turn right onto Tutukau Rd for 13 km, then left on to Orakei Korako Rd, T07-378 3131, orakeikorako.co.nz.Open 0800-1630, $36, child $15.*
About 40 km north of Taupo is one of the least visited, but best thermal parks in the country. From the lakeside visitor centre only plumes of steam and a colourful silica terrace across the water give any indication of the numerous interesting volcanic features awaiting you. Once delivered at the terraces by boat you are free to roam the self-guided tracks of the reserve. There is a bit of everything here including algae-covered silica terraces, boiling pools, geysers and bubbly mud.

Taupo and around listings

For hotel and restaurant price codes and other relevant information, see pages 9-14.

⬤ Where to stay

Taupo *p69, map p71*
$$$ Terraces Hotel, Napier-Taupo Highway, T07-378 7080, terraceshotel. co.nz. First established in 1889 this hotel on the edge of the town has standard rooms, studio suites, bar and restaurant that combined offer both class and character. The added attraction is the Hot Springs and Spa Resort only a short stroll away.
$$-$ Action Downunder YHA Hostel, 56 Kaimanawa St, T07-3783311, yha.co.nz. A very tidy YHA associate with great modern rooms and facilities including family and double en suites with personal computer and internet – a rare find. Off-street parking, impressive kitchen facilities, outdoor big-screen movies, spa, gym and bike hire.

Motor parks
$$$-$ De Brett's Thermal Resort, Napier/Taupo Highway (SH5), T07-378 8559, debrettsresort.co.nz. A well-facilitated 5-star motor park located right opposite the hot pools complex at the edge of town. Standard and self-contained cabins, studio and family units and lodges. Powered and non-powered sites, camp kitchen and TV lounge. Concession rates to thermal pools are an added incentive.
$ Wairakei Thermal Valley Motor Camp, Wairakei, T07-374 8004. Basic camping with powered sites and camp kitchen 9 km north of Taupo and 1.5 km from SH1. The appeal here is the peaceful location and the small menagerie of visitor-loving animals roaming free.

⬤ Restaurants

Taupo *p69, map p71*
$$$ The Brantry Restaurant, 45 Rifle Range Rd, Taupo, T07-378 0484. Owned and operated by local sisters Prue and Felicity Campbell the Brantry is fast earning a reputation as one of Taupo's best. Set in a stylishly refurbished 1950s town house you can enjoy the intimacy of the cellar room or the buzz of alfresco in summer. Beautifully presented and affordable contemporary NZ cuisine and an extensive wine list. Perhaps try the set 3-course option and for sweet the divine Tiramisu.
$$ L'Arte Mosaic café and Sculpture Garden, 225 Marapa Rd, Acacia Bay (2.5 km off Acacia Bay Rd right on to Marapa Rd), T07-378 2962. Wed-Sun 0900-1600. A magical little café that has grown around the work and imaginations of local clay artist Judi Brennan. Her signature quirky clay garden decor adorned with colourful mosaics and the work of other local artists are a delight and the food and coffee is also well worth the trip. Try the famous 'eggs benny'.

⬤ What to do

Taupo *p69, map p71*
Skydives
Taupo Tandem, Taupo, T07-377 0428, T0800-275934, taupotandemskydiving. com. One of 3 companies in New Zealand's capital of the tandem skydive.

⬤ Directory

Taupo *p69, map p71*
Hospital Kotare St, T07-376 1000; Taupo Medical Centre, corner of Heu Heu and Kaimanawa streets, T07-3784080.
Pharmacy Mainstreet Open Late Pharmacy, corner Tongariro St and Heuheu St, Taupo, T07-3782636, 0900-2030.

Tongariro National Park

Tongariro National Park is New Zealand's oldest national park, and the fourth oldest in the world. In 1887 Horonuku Te Heuheu Tukino, the then paramount chief of Ngati Tuwharetoa, gave the central portion – essentially the volcanoes of Ruapehu, Ngauruhoe and Tongariro – to the nation. In more recent years the park has been substantially increased in size to cover an area of 75,250 ha, taking in the forest, tussock country and volcanic desert to the east. The slopes of Ruapehu serve as the principal North Island base for skiing in winter and in summer the park offers excellent walking opportunities, including the Tongariro Crossing, hailed as the best one-day walk in the country.

Visiting Tongariro National Park

Getting around

The park is bordered along its north and western sides by the SH47 and to the east by SH1 – the famous Desert Road. Whakapapa Village, at the northern base of Ruapehu, serves as the park's main headquarters.

A number of local operators service the Tongariro National Park and Tongariro Crossing, daily via Turangi, Whakapapa and National Park, including (from Taupo) **Tongariro Expeditions** ⓘ *T07-377 0435, thetongarirocrossing.co.nz*; **Alpine Hotbus** ⓘ *T0508468287, alpinehotbus.co.nz* and (from Ohakune) **Maitai Shuttles** ⓘ *T06-385 8724, tongarirocrossingtransport.co.nz*.

Bus station The i-SITE in Turangi is the principal bus arrival and departure point. They can assist with local and national bus and coach ticketing.

Tourist information

Turangi i-SITE visitor centre ⓘ *Ngawaka Pl, just off SH1, T07-3868999, laketaupo nz.com, ruapehunz.com, daily 0830-1730*. **DoC Whakapapa** ⓘ *Whakapapa Village on SH48, T07-892 3729, doc.govt.nz, whakapapa.co.nz, mtruapehu.com, daily 0800-1700*, has a wealth of information on the park, interesting displays, maps and weather reports. **Ruapehu i-SITE visitor centre** ⓘ *54 Clyde St, Ohakune, T06-385 8427, ohakune.info, visitruapehu.com, Mon-Fri 0900-1700, Sat-Sun 0900-1530 (summer)*. For a live webcam of Ngauruhoe or Ruapehu visit geonet.org.nz/volcano/animations/ngauruhoe.html; and geonet.org.nz/volcano/animations/ruapehu.html.

The park

All of the national park's sights are, of course, natural and dominated by the three majestic volcanic peaks of Ngauruhoe, Ruapehu and Tongariro. Although all three mountains are active volcanoes they are quite different in size and appearance.

The symmetrical cone of Ngauruhoe (2291 m) is the youngest of the three volcanoes. Its classic cone shape is due to its relative youth, but also because it has a single vent, unlike Ruapehu and Tongariro. Although Ruapehu has been far more active recently, Ngauruhoe has, over the years, been considered the most continuously active, frequently venting steam and gas and, occasionally, ash and lava. Its last significant eruption occurred in 1954. About 16 km south of Ngauruhoe is the majestic shape of Ruapehu, with its truncated cone, perpetually snow-covered summit peaks and crater lake. It is the North Island's highest mountain, at 2797 m, and over the course of the last century has seen the most violent activity of all the three volcanoes. Between 1945 and 1947, due to a number of eruptions blocking the overflow, the waters of the craterlake rose dramatically. On the stormy Christmas Eve of 1953, without warning, the walls of the crater collapsed and a mighty lahar (volcanic rock and water debris) rushed down the Whangaehu River, wiping out the rail bridge near Karioi. The night train to Auckland arrived moments later and 153 lives were lost. It erupted more recently in September 1995, miraculously without loss of life, and the same thing happened a year later, wiping out the possibility of a ski season for both Whakapapa and Turoa. Ruapehu attracts thousands of visitors each year who come to ski or climb, or enjoy its numerous tramping tracks. Both the summit and Crater Lake of Ruapehu are popular climbs and are, in part, easily accessible via the Whakapapa Ski Field chairlift. The climb to the crater and back takes about seven hours (four hours if you use the chairlifts). Whatever your intentions, always obtain all the necessary information before attempting this climb, go well prepared and do not go alone. Ruapehu is home to two main ski fields: Whakapapa on its northwestern flank (serviced by Whakapapa village) and Turoa on the southwestern flank (serviced by Ohakune). Whakapapa is home to the area's most prominent man-made feature, the gracious Bayview Chateau Hotel built in 1929.

Tongariro, at the northern fringe 3 km north of Ngauruhoe, is a fairly complex, flat topped affair and the lowest at 1968 m. Of the three mountains until recently it was seen as the most benign, having lain dormant for over a century. However, on 7 August 2012 it erupted, sending up an ash cloud but causing no injuries. At the time of going to press experts were commenting that it was too early to say whether the eruption marked the beginning of a new period of volcanic activity. From a purely aesthetic point of view its most attractive features are the aptly named Red Crater (which is still active) and the small Emerald Lakes at its base. Nearby are the contrasting Blue Lakes of the central crater and the Ketetahi Springs (hot, but no access is allowed), which emerge on its northern slopes.

Tongariro Crossing

Providing the weather is kind, there is no doubt that the views and the varied volcanic features certainly make this excellent walk a memorable one. But to call it a walk is really an understatement: at about 16 km in length with some steep climbs and the odd bit of scrambling, it is really a mountain hike that can take up to 10 hours. In winter it can be impassable and even in summer it can be dangerous, so despite what you may have heard, don't underestimate it. Having said that, provided you are fit, well prepared and the weather is looking good, you should not pass up the opportunity. One other word of warning. In summer and on a clear day don't expect to be alone; the track now has to handle more than a 1000 people a day, which can spoil it a little. Given the recent eruption of Tongariro Volcano (see above), seek advice on the walk before setting out.

The walk can be tackled from either north or south, with a number of diversions on the way. The usual recommendation is to start from the Mangatepopo Car Park (off SH47 on the park's western edge) at dawn, and walk the 16 km straight to the SH47A at the park's northern edge (walk terminus) by late afternoon. Much depends on your transport and whether you are tied in to organized drop-offs or are independent. If relying on the various shuttle buses unfortunately in summer you really cannot escape the crowds. However, if you have your own transport try ascending from the northern flank (Ketetahi). Start one hour before dawn (with a head torch) and then you will reach the great vistas at dawn and essentially be alone. The ant trails of people start appearing on the southern horizon about 1000.

From south to north (Mangatepopo) the track makes a gradual ascent towards the southern slopes of Tongariro, while the steep slopes and lava flows of Ngauruhoe loom to the northwest. Sandwiched between the two mountains the track is then forced to make a steep ascent up the Mangatepopo Saddle. Before this ascent there is the option of a short diversion to the Soda Springs – a series of cold springs that emerge from beneath an old lava flow, surrounded by an oasis of greenery. Once you have negotiated the Saddle you enter Tongariro's South Crater. The views of Ngauruhoe from here are excellent (and the especially fit can take in the summit diversion from here). A short climb then leads to the aptly named Red Crater and the highest point on the crossing (1886 m). Following the rim of this colourful (and, in the odd place, steaming) crater you are then treated to a full artist's palette, with the partial descent to the Emerald Lakes, which make food colouring seem bland. (The minerals from Red Crater create the colours in the water). Just beyond Emerald Lakes the track branches right to Oturere Hut, or continues to Ketetahi Hut across the Central Crater and alongside Blue Lake, another water-filled vent. The track then straddles the North Crater taking in the stunning view north across Lake Taupo, before making a gradual zigzag descent to the Ketetahi Hut. The hut sits alone on the slopes at an altitude of about 1000 m, like a first-class real estate property: location, location, location and a real view. (It is the busiest and most popular hut in the park. If you have booked your stay in the hut bear in mind it operates on a first-come first-served basis, so get there early.) The huts all have mattresses, gas cookers (summer only), water supplies and toilet facilities. In the busy seasons wardens can provide information and weather reports. The hot Ketetahi Springs are on private Maori land only a few hundred metres away. Years ago a soak in the pools of the stream armed with a gin and tonic was a highlight of the walk. But sadly disagreements between DOC and the local Iwi mean the springs and stream are now out of bounds. From Ketetahi it is a two-hour descent through native bush to the SH47A access point. For more information contact the DoC Whakapapa visitor centre, page 63.

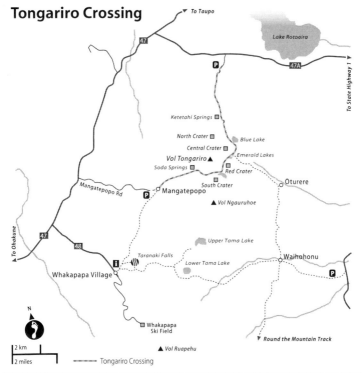

Tongariro Crossing

Tongariro National Park listings

For hotel and restaurant price codes and other relevant information, see pages 9-14.

Where to stay

Tongariro National Park *p74, map p77*
$$$$-$$ Bayview Chateau, Whakapapa Village, T07-892 3809, chateau.co.nz. Perhaps the most famous hotel in the North Island, the Bayview provides traditional luxury in a grand location. Visible for miles around, the hotel sits like a beacon in the heart of the national park. Elegance in keeping with its age (1929) combined with traditional modern facilities, including an excellent restaurant, a bar, café, pool and even a golf course.
$$$ Powderhorn Chateau, corner of Mangawhero and Thames streets, Ohakune, T06-385 8888, powderhorn. co.nz. Alpine-style accommodation base especially for skiing in winter. Choice of lodge-style suites, an apartment, a heated swimming pool and a small casino. Warm and lively atmosphere in the bar and 2 in-house restaurants. Ski and bike hire is also available.

Motor parks
$$-$ Whakapapa Holiday Park, Whakapapa Village, T07-892 3897, whakapapa.net.nz. Standard motor park and backpacker accommodation with basic facilities but set in the heart of the village and riverside close to all amenities.

Restaurants

Tongariro National Park *p74, map p77*
$$-$ Knoll Ridge Café, top of the Bruce Rd (take the chairlift!), Whakapapa, T07-892 3738. Chairlift $21, child $11. Open 0900-1600 (last lift down 1600 in summer). This is the highest café in the North Island, at the top of the main chairlifts of the Whakapapa ski field. Not only a good place to head if you fancy a coffee with a view, but the ride is wonderful and you can take a walk to the ridgeline for even better views. For conditions, refer to mtruapehu.com.

What to do

Tongariro National Park *p74, map p77*
Extreme adventures
Mokai Gravity Canyon, Taihape (look for signs 7 km south of the town), T06-388 9109/T0800 802864, gravitycanyon.co.nz. The Mokai Canyon site on the Rangitikei River near Taihape boasts 3 extreme adventure activities. The 1-km flying fox, an 80-m bungee and a 50-m freefall on a bridge swing. Great even for spectators.

Skiing
Whakapapa and Turoa
Ski fields, full winter program and facilities but also interesting summer activities. See mtruapehu.com.

Transport

Tongariro National Park *p74, map p77*
See Visiting Tongariro National Park, page 75.

Waikato and the Waitomo Caves

The Waikato is one of the country's richest agricultural areas, where the eponymous river – the longest in the country – snakes its way through a landscape of green rolling hills and fields. The Waikato, the homeland of the Tainui people – one of the largest tribes in the land – is rich in Maori history, as well as being home to the current Maori queen and head of state. The first Maori king was elected here in 1858 and the subsequent formation of the Maori King Movement, in direct opposition to rule under the British monarchy, led to much bloodshed. After almost a year of fierce battles and confrontation the British finally quashed the Kingites, who fled to southern Waikato, which is now also known as King Country. Today, peace reigns, but the memory lives on.

Waikato also boasts New Zealand's fourth largest city, Hamilton. Although not a major tourist destination, the Waikato is a region with considerable diversity from the famous surf beaches on its coast to the jewel in the crown of the King Country, the Waitomo District, a wonderland of limestone caves and subterranean activities that deservedly make it one of the North Island's premier tourist attractions.

Visiting Waikato and the Waitomo Caves

Getting around
Both SH1 and the main Auckland to Wellington trunk rail line run through the heart of the Waikato. In Hamilton regional buses arrive and depart from the **Transport Centre** (and i-SITE) ① *corner of Bryce and Anglesea streets, T07-834 3457/T07-839 3580*. For information on local bus services, contact **Busit** ① *T0800-42875463, busit.co.nz*. The **train station** ① *is on Fraser St, in Frankton T0800-872467, tranzscenic.co.nz*.

To get to the Waitomo Caves by bus, the **Waitomo Shuttle** ① *T0800-808279, $12 one-way*, operates a regular service from 0900-1730, between Otorohanga and Waitomo. The **Waitomo Wanderer** ① *T03-477 9083/T0508-926337, waitomotours.co.nz, $45 ($75 return)*, runs a daily service from Rotorua. It departs Rotorua at 0745 and arrives in Waitomo at 1000, departing Waitomo again at 1545. All the major bus companies offer transport and tours to the glow-worm cave from Auckland and Rotorua; shop around for the best deal. If coming by car or motor home, note there is no fuel available in Waitomo village.

Tourist information

Hamilton i-SITE visitor centre ① *Hamilton Transport Centre, corner of Bryce and Anglesea streets, T07-839 3580, visithamilton.co.nz, waikatonz.co.nz, Mon-Thu 0715-1730, Fri 0715-1845, Sat 0900-1645, Sun 0930-1845.* **Otorohanga i-SITE visitor centre** ① *on the main SH drag at 21 Maniapoto St, T07-873 8951, otorohanga.co.nz, Mon-Fri 0900-1730, Sat-Sun 1000-1600.* **Waitomo Museum of Caves i-SITE visitor centre** ① *T0800-474839/T07-878 7640, waitomo.org.nz and waitomo-museum.co.nz, daily 0845-1930.*

Hamilton

Perched on the serpentine banks of the famous Waikato River, 129 km south of Auckland, Hamilton is the main service centre for the rich fertile agricultural region of the Waikato. Being so close to the major tourist destinations of Auckland and Rotorua, the city struggles to attract visitors for any length of time as it has few major attractions. It is, however, ideally located for explorations around the Waikato Region and can be used as base for exploring the North Island. Visitors stopping briefly in the city can enjoy a visit the celebrated museum, gardens and free-flight aviary of Hamilton Zoo.

Waikato Coast

With the well-advertised attractions of Waitomo and its caves, the Waikato Coast seldom features very high on the average travelling agenda. Indeed, after some unique subterranean adventures most simply pass through the Waikato on the way south, or east to the capital of all things thermal – Rotorua. But for those with more time, who wish to ride a world-class left-hand break, or who simply wish to get off the beaten track, then the Waikato Coast offers some pleasant surprises. The small laid-back coastal village of **Raglan**, 50 km west of Hamilton, offers a palpable sense of relaxation, not to mention plenty of the near legendary surf breaks. Further south, a diversion off SH1 to the remote coastal village of **Kawhia**, and back via the **Marakopa Falls** to Waitomo, can be a relaxing, scenic and often solitary highlight.

Otorohanga

The small agricultural service town of Oto, as it is better known, fancies itself as the gateway to the caves and boasts one of the best kiwi houses and displays of native New Zealand birds in the country at the **Otorohanga Kiwi House and Native Bird Park** ① *Alex Telfer Dr, T07-8737391, kiwihouse.org.nz, daily 0900-1630, $20, child $6.*

But before heading off to Waitomo or making a beeline for the kiwi house it is also worth looking at the **Kiwiana Displays** at various points along the main street. They are very well presented and chronicle a range of kiwi icons, heritage and heroes from Sir Edmund Hillary to rugby and Pavlova. The i-SITE visitor centre has a locations leaflet, which comes with a quiz.

Waitomo and the caves

Heading south, beyond the gentle meanderings of the Waikato River and the uninspiring urban vistas of Hamilton, the rest of the Waikato is typical of the North Island countryside with deliciously green, gently rolling hills replete with plump and contented dairy cows. However, in these parts, perhaps more than anywhere else in the country, looks are deceiving since beneath the hooves and the haystacks exists a very different world more suited to the stuff of mystical dreams and wild adventures. As Rotorua is to bubbly mud or Kaikoura is to whales, then southern Waikato and Waitomo are to subterranean caves,

Waitomo Walkway

If the idea of disappearing underground for a few hours wearing a wetsuit, a rubber ring and a miner's torch holds little appeal then try The Waitomo Walkway (three hours return). No wetsuit, no rubber ring, no worms with glowing bottoms, just a good pair of walkie boots. It begins opposite Glow-worm Cave and follows the Waitomo Stream, taking in a number of limestone features before arriving at the Ruakuri Scenic Reserve.

This reserve encompasses a short walk that is hailed as one of New Zealand's best. Although it does not deserve quite that billing, it is well worth it, with a circular track taking in interesting caves and natural limestone bridges, hidden amongst lush, native bush. At night, just before the path crosses the stream, you can see a small 'scintilla' of glow-worms. These are the only glow-worms you'll see around here for free.

rivers and glow-worms. There is easy access to a labyrinth of incredible limestone caves and underground river systems and to all the unique activities that go with them. Where else for example can you abseil 100 m into the 'Lost World' or float through the 'Haggas Honking Holes'?

The district of Waitomo ('wai' water and 'tomo' hole) is one of the North Island's biggest tourist attractions. Below ground there is an astonishing network of over 360 recorded caves in the area, the longest over 14 km. If you don't mind getting wet, you should promise yourself that you will try at least one of the amazing underground activities, beyond the highly commercial tour of the Glow-worm cave. Wherever you go, it is pretty unforgettable. All the various companies are based in or around the small village of Waitomo. Waitomo Museum of Caves i-SITE visitor centre is at the heart of operations and almost all the above-ground attractions; below-ground activity operators, booking offices and tourist amenities are within walking distance. Although compact it can be confusing, so the best bet is to absorb the information at the i-SITE and take your time. There are numerous and often very similar activities on offer. Let the staff book on your behalf, or go to the relevant tour operator for more information. The i-SITE has internet access and currency exchange. There is also an ATM outside.

Waikato and the Waitomo Caves listings

For hotel and restaurant price codes and other relevant information, see pages 9-14.

🛏 Where to stay

Hamilton *p80*
$$$-$ Solscape, located 7 km west of Raglan village centre at 611 Wainui Rd, T07-825 8268, solscape.co.nz. Again, if you're looking for something completely different this really is the only place to stay in Raglan 35 km west of Hamilton. The owners have gone to great pains to relocate and

renovate an array of railway wagons as colourful accommodation units from dorm to self-contained. Smaller cabooses (cabin houses) and a choice of 3 fully self-contained cottages (2 with open fires), powered and tent sites are also available. Bay views and a veritable menagerie of animals add to the appeal.

Waitomo and the caves *p80*
$$$ Waitomo Express and Hobbit Motel, 1177 Waitomo Valley Rd, Waitomo, T07-8786666, woodlynpark.co.nz. If it is the

unusual you are looking for, look no further than Barry Woods at Woodlyn Park (1 km down Waitomo Valley Rd) and his converted train carriage, hobbit motel, or ex-Second World War aircraft and patrol boat accommodation. Most are self-contained.

Motor parks
$$$-$ Waitomo Caves Top Ten Holiday Park, Waitomo T07-878 7639, waitomopark. co.nz. A modern, convenient and very friendly motor camp right in the heart of the village. Spacious, great facilities including internet, pool and spa.

⑦ Restaurants

Hamilton *p80*
$$ Scott's Epicurean, 181 Victoria St, T07-839 6680. Daily Mon-Fri from 0700 for breakfast, lunch. Sat/Sun from 0830 for brunch. Hamilton is renowned for its wide range of quality eateries and it is hard to choose, but this long-established funky little café with its imaginative lunch/brunch menu is hard to resist.

Waitomo and the caves *p80*
$$ Waitomo Caves Tavern, near the i-SITE visitor centre, Waitomo Village, T07-878 8448. The great place to go for cheap and basic pub grub and a pint with the locals.

⑥ Entertainment

Waitomo and the caves *p80*
Woodlyn Park, 1177 Waitomo Valley Rd, T07-878 6666, woodlynpark.co.nz. $26,
child $15. Shows at 1130 and 1330. This is the above-ground entertainment must-see in Waitomo, if not the region. A typical example of Kiwi imagination, ingenuity and that simple can-do mentality. The show, hosted by ex-shearer Barry Woods or staff, is an informative, interactive (and at times comical) interpretation of old and modern-day Kiwi country life, and is hard to describe You'll just have to go and see for yourself.

❹ What to do

Waitomo and the caves *p80*
Waitomo Adventures, T0800-924866/07-878 7788, waitomo.co.nz. If you can afford it try the 7-hr **Lost World Epic**. With a 100 m abseil and 5 hrs underground this is one of the best and most unusual full-day activity trips in the country.

❺ Transport

Waitomo and the caves *p80*
There is a domestic **airport** at Hamilton.
There are south/north bound **bus services** from Auckland to Hamilton. Waitomo is served from **Auckland, Hamilton, Otorohanga, Taupo** and **Rotorua**. The main i-SITES can assist with schedules and bookings.
There is a daily **train service** from **Auckland** to **Wellington** stopping at Hamilton and Otorohanga (for Waitomo).
See also Visiting Waikato and the Waitomo Caves, page 79.

Bay of Plenty and East Cape

When Captain James Cook explored this particular stretch of the country's coast in the 18th century he christened it the Bay of Plenty. Back then a mere stretch of the legs on terra firma was no doubt enough to attain such a label. But now, for us modern-day navigators, the obvious question remains – so, is it?

Well, if statistics are anything to go by the answer is categorically yes. By population, the Bay of Plenty is the North Island's fastest-growing region, with the real estate figures of Tauranga now generally accepted as being a barometer to the health of the national economy. Of course inland Rotorua steals most of the attention – and the visitors – but if you have time to spare, a little exploration along the coast here can be rewarding, especially given the almost irresistible attraction of White Island, which is currently the most active volcano in the country.

Visiting Bay of Plenty and East Cape

Getting around
Tauranga, 210 km southeast of Auckland and 83 km north of Rotorua. Regional buse
arrive and depart from the i-SITES in Tauranga and Whakatane; all handle bookings and
ticketing. **Bayline Coaches** (Bay Hopper) ① *T07-578 3113/T0800-422 9287, baylinebus
co.nz*, is the local suburban bus company operating regular daily services to Rotorua
Mount Maunganui and east as far as Opotiki.

Tourist information
Tauranga i-SITE visitor centre ① *95 Willow St, T07-578 8103, bayofplentynz.com, Mon-Fr
0830-1730, Sat-Sun 0900-1700.* **Mount Maunganui i-SITE visitor centre** ① *Salisbury Av
T07-575 5099, Mon-Fri 0900-1700, Sat/Sun 0900-1600.* **Whakatane i-SITE visitor centre**
① *corner of Quay Dr and Kakahoroa Dr (east of the centre), T07-308 6058, whakatane.com
Dec-Feb Mon-Fri 0800-1800, Sat/Sun 0900-1700, Mar-Nov Mon-Fri 0800-1700, Sat/Sun 1000-
1600.* **Opotiki i-SITE visitor centre** ① *corner of St John and Elliot streets, T07-315 3031
opotikinz.com, daily 0800-1700.*

Tauranga
Tauranga has enjoyed tremendous growth in recent years. With the combination o
location, climate, attractive beaches and the many associated activities, as well as its
proximity to the delights of Rotorua, it has much to offer both the native and the tourist
Dominating the scene is the harbour and the volcanic dome of Mount Maunganui to the
north, which guards its precarious entrance. Nowadays there are almost as many cruise
liners as there are merchant ships, and the town's tourist allure seems almost set to
overtake its popularity with the locals.

The main historical attraction in Tauranga is the **Elms Mission House** ① *Mission St, T07-
577 9772, theelms.org.nz, Wed, Sat, Sun 1400-1600, $5*, set amidst pleasant grounds on the
Te Papa Peninsula, on the site of the original mission.

Of a more contemporary nature is the chic **Tauranga Art Gallery** ① *corner of Willow and
Wharf streets, T07-578 7933 art gallery.org.nz*, which is well worth a look around.

Mount Maunganui
Six kilometres north of Tauranga and dominated by the Mount, the town of Mount
Maunganui is graced by golden beaches and maintains an irresistible appeal to kiwi
holidaymakers. In winter the streets and beaches are almost empty, but in summer and
particularly over the New Year, the town is a tourist battleground with the Mount crowned
with an army of view junkies and the beach with battalions of soporific sunbathers.
Mount Maunganui itself (known as 'Mauao' or '**The Mount**') is 232 m high and dominates
the coastal horizon at the narrow entrance to Tauranga Harbour. There is a network of
pathways that criss-cross the Mount, offering a range of pleasant walks to suit all levels of
fitness. The summit climb takes about 45 minutes, while the 3.5-km base track walk is a less
demanding option and also offers some good views. At the base of the mount is the **Mount
Maunganui Hot Salt Water Pools** ① *Adams Av, T07-5750868, tcal.co.nz/Facilities/mount
hotpools.html, Mon-Sat 0600-2200, Sun 0800-2200, $10.40, child $7.80*, where therapeutic
salt water is heated to 39°C in a number of large communal and private pools.

From the narrow neck of the Mount, **Ocean Beach** begins a stretch of sand that sweeps,
almost uninterrupted, east to Whakatane.

Whakatane

Whakatane is the principal town in the eastern Bay of Plenty, at the mouth of the Whakatane River. It has a vibrant atmosphere that is often lacking in many New Zealand towns of the same size. Whakatane is rich in Maori history, with settlement taking place before the great migrations of the 14th century. For the modern tourist Whakatane serves principally as a gateway to visit the active volcano White Island, which can, on a clear day, be seen 50 km offshore, steaming away merrily. The other major activities are swimming with dolphins, fishing, diving (again off White Island) and, to a lesser extent, walking in the Urewera National and Whirinaki Forest parks.

Ohope

Just 8 km over the hill from Whakatane, heading east, is the 11-km-long sandspit called Ohope Beach, guarding the entrance to the Ohiwa Harbour. Principally a beach resort, it is a fine place to while away a few hours in the sun, swimming, sunbathing or just watching White Island billow with steam in the distance.

White Island

A distinctly steamy affair White Island (Whakāri) is one of New Zealand's most active cone volcanoes built up by continuous volcanic activity over the past 150,000 years. What makes it more remarkable is that about 70% of the volcano is under the sea, making this massive volcanic structure one of the largest in New Zealand. Captain Cook christened it White Island in 1769 purely due to its appearance. But he apparently did not come close enough to confirm, or even realize it was a volcano.

As well as a fascinating natural and geological history it also has a fascinating human history that revolves principally around sulphur mining, which began on the island in 1885. Quite what mining sulphur must have been like on an active volcano in the late 1800s blows the mind (if you'll pardon the pun). This was surely the domain of either desperate or greedy men. In 1914 part of the crater wall collapsed and the resulting landslide destroyed the sulphur mine and miners' village with twelve lives lost and that, as they say, was that. Along with the fascinating and colourful natural features that range from steaming vents, fumaroles and that wonderful 'what if' feeling, what remains of the buildings from that era are now a major tourist attraction. The island is now privately owned and became a private scenic reserve in 1953. Daily tours allow more than 10,000 people to visit White Island every year and GeoNet constantly monitors volcanic activity. The most recent eruption was in 2000 when a new vent developed and began to emit ash. An eruption then occurred late in July, which covered the crater area in scoria, also displacing the main craterlake and forming a new explosion crater 150 m across. Of course these days although subtle changes can occur at any time and you can never say never, it is perfectly safe to visit and were any major eruption imminent all the monitoring would almost certainly provide ample warning. One thing however that is a tad amusing is that all visitors must wear a hard hat.

You can visit the island by boat or by helicopter. The principal (and very good) water-based tour company is **Pee Jays** ① *15 Strand East, Whakatane, T07-3089588, T0800-733529, whiteisland.co.nz*. They offer excellent five-to six-hour volcano trips with around two hour on the island. Lunch and refreshments provided. It will often deviate off schedule if dolphins are spotted, $199. Bookings essential.

By helicopter try **Vulcan Helicopters** ① *T0800-804354, vulcanheli.co.nz*. It takes 2½ hours, including a guided tour of the island, $550.

East Cape to Gisborne

Those with a healthy imagination and good sense of geography will recognize East Cape a the heel of the upside-down boot that is New Zealand. East Cape is the least-visited area i the North Island. This is due not so much to its isolated location but its geography. Almos the entire peninsula is sparsely populated, remote and mountainous. Indeed, much of the Raukumara Range, which makes up most of its interior, remains impenetrable by road with only wild rivers like the Motu and Mata carving their way through the wilderness Many make the trip to experience a sunrise at the Cape Lighthouse and satisfy themselves they are one of the first on that day to see it. Of course whether you can depends on the cloud cover but it does add a unique aspect to the trip.

Further south and back to civilization the coastal town of Gisborne prides itself on being the first place Captain Cook set foot in New Zealand in 1769 and in modern times good surf breaks and winemaking. Inland from Wairoa (south of Gisborne) and the enchanting Mahia Peninsula, are the dense forests of the Te Urewera National Park, a place of almos spiritual beauty and particularly famous for its Great Walk, which circumnavigates its mos scenic jewel, Lake Waikaremoana.

The best way to explore the Cape is undoubtedly to drive the 331 km of SH35 from either Opotiki to Gisborne or vice versa. Although the trip can be done comfortably in two days, taking longer will allow you to soak up the laid-back atmosphere and explore the numerous bays and beaches as you go.

Before embarking on the trip pick up the detailed road guide from the **Opotiki i-SITE** ① *corner St John and Elliott St, Opotiki, T07-315 3031, infocentre@odc.govt.nz/opotikinz.com open Mon-Fri 0800-1600, Sat-Sun 0930-1330.*

Gisborne

The agricultural service town, port and coastal resort of Gisborne attracts many visitors in search of the sun, eager to jump on a surfboard or explore the East Cape. Being the most easterly city in the country, Gisborne prides itself on being the first city in the world to see the sunrise. It is also the first place that Captain Cook set foot in New Zealand in October 1769. Given that it might be rude not to visit **Cook's Landing Site and National Historic Reserve** next to the main port and the base of Titirangi (Kaiti Hill). To get there, cross to the east bank of the river, which flows through the centre of the town. The reserve marks the spot where Cook first set foot to a hostile response from local Maori. Above the reserve the Kaiti Hill provides great views across the city and the second of three Cook memorial edifices. Set in trees at the foot of the hill to the east is the **Te Poho-O-Rawiri marae**, which was built in 1930 and is one of the largest carved meeting houses in the country.

To see the third Cook memorial and a statue of Cook's cabin boy, Young Nick (who is credited as being the first to sight land), head to the beachside reserve on the southern bank of the river. These statues are of particular interest simply because of their location with the backdrop of the port and huge steel-hulled cargo ships, which prove we have come a long way since the tall ships and crow's nests.

For a comprehensive insight in to local and regional history head for the **Gisborne Museum** (Tairawhiti) ① *Stout St, T06-867 3832, tairawhitimuseum.org.nz, Mon-Sat 1000-1600, Sun 1330-1600, donation.*

There are an ever-increasing number of **vineyards** around the region producing the notable vintages. Contact the **i-SITE visitor centre** ① *209 Grey St, Gisborne, T06 868-6139.*

For information relating to Lake Waikaremoana and Te Urewera National Park contact the **DoC visitor centre** ① *T06-837 3803, doc.govt.nz.*

Urewera National Park and Lake Waikaremoana

Te Urewera is daunting and mysterious; a place of almost threatening beauty. The national park encompasses the largest area of native bush in the North Island and is the third largest national park in the country. The main focus of the park is Lake Waikaremoana, the Sea of Rippling Waters, while the track, which circumnavigates it, the Lake Waikaremoana Circuit, is one of the most popular walks in the North Island. The area has a fascinating natural and human history and the vast park is home to a wealth of wildlife: some native and welcome including kiwi, kaka and kokako (one of New Zealand's rarest and most endangered birds). The hub for amenities and accommodation surrounds the motor camp and DoC visitor centre in Waikaremoana. There you can plan some excellent short bush walks, or if time allows the full circuit; a 46-km walk of moderate difficulty, that can usually be completed in three to four days. It can be walked at any time of year and has excellent hut facilities, but permits must be obtained from the **DoC Aniwaniwa visitor centre** ① *SH38 at Lake Waikaremoana, T06-837 3803, urewerainfo@doc.govt.nz, daily 1000-1700.* Staff can assist with the limited but surprisingly good accommodation options and also handle walk information, fees and hut bookings.

Wairoa is the eastern gateway to the Te Urewera National Park and sits on the coast at the junction of SH2 and SH36, roughly halfway between Gisborne (98 km) and Napier (118 km). Access to Lake Waikaremoana and the heart of the park is 61 km via the hardy SH38. From Waikaremoana it is then a further 75 km to Murupara, or 137 km to Rotorua. If accessing the park from the east call in at the **Wairoa i-SITE visitor centre** ① *corner of SH2 and Queen Street, T06-838 7440/0800 924762, wairoanz.com.*

Bay of Plenty and East Cape listings

For hotel and restaurant price codes and other relevant information, see pages 9-14.

⊙ Where to stay

Tauranga *p84*
$$$-$$ Harbour City Motor Inn, 50 Wharf St, T07-571 1435, taurangaharbourcity.co.nz. Modern motel, ideally located in the heart of Tauranga. Stylish studio and 2-bedroom units with spa. Sky TV and parking.

Mount Maunganui *p84*
Motor parks
$$$-$ Top Ten Papamoa Beach Holiday Resort, 535 Papamoa Beach Rd, T07-572 0816, papamoabeach.co.nz. One of many options and a good base near Mt Maunganui. Beachfront location with a wide range of accommodation options and facilities.

Whakatane *p85*
$$$-$$ White Island Rendezvous, 15 Strand East, T0800-733529, T07-308 9500, whiteisland.co.nz. Part of the Pee Jay White Island tour operation, so ideal if you are taking the tour. Modern waterfront motel with a full range of units from standard to deluxe with spa, a fully self-contained apartment and cottage. Sky TV and internet ports. Café open 0630-1700.

East Cape to Gisborne *p86*
$$ Waiwaka B&B and Snapper Bach, located 2 km north of Te Kaha and 12 km from Whanarua Bay, East Cape T07-325 2070, waikawa.net. Modern self-contained 2-bedroom bach and separate bed and breakfast en suites in a peaceful spot. TV, BBQ, cooking facilities, internet.

Gisborne p86
Motor parks
$$$ Morere Hot Springs Accommodation,
SH2, Morere, (52 km south of Gisborne)
T06-837 8824, morerehotsprings.co.nz.
Lodge (6 bedrooms) plus 2 character self-
contained cabins and cottage. Just a short
stroll from the hot springs.
$$$-$ Waikanae Beach Holiday Park,
Grey St, T06-867 5634, gisborneholidaypark.
co.nz. This is the best-equipped and most
centrally located motor camp in town. Short
walk to the beach and i-SITE visitor centre.

Restaurants

Tauranga p84
$$$ Harbourside Restaurant, The Strand,
T0800-721714, harbourside-tga.co.nz. Open
1130-late. Enjoys a loyal following and the
reputation as Tauranga's best restaurant.
Located as much on the water as beside
it, at the southern end of the Strand, it
offers an excellent and imaginative all-day
blackboard and à la carte menu, with an
emphasis on the NZ contemporary classics
and local seafood.

Mount Maunganui p84
$$$-$$ Astrolabe, 82 Maunganui Rd,
T07-574 8155, astrolabe.co.nz. Open for
breakfast, lunch and dinner. Named not
after a space ship, but a shipwreck, this
classy combination restaurant, bar and café
offers breakfast, lunch and dinner with a
range of fine and imaginative traditional
dishes. Live bands often play at weekends.

Gisborne p86
$$$-$$ The Wharf Café, 60 The Esplanade,
The Wharf, T06-868 4876, wharfbar.co.nz.
Daily 0900-late. This is not very expensive
but still at the high end, very popular, with

wide-ranging menu with European, Pacific
Rim and Asian combinations. Nautically
themed and a great waterside setting
overlooking the marina.
**$$ Colosseum Café and Wine Bar
(Matawhero Wines)**, Riverpoint Rd,
Matawhero, 10 mins from Gisborne,
T06-868 8366. Open Mon-Sat.Excellent
vineyard option attached to the Matawhero
Vineyard where established vintner Denis
Irwin has, since the mid-1970s, earned a
fine reputation for his gewurztraminers.
Also produced are Chardonnay, Cabernet
Sauvignon, Merlot and Pinot Noir.

What to do

Mount Maunganui p84
Surfing
Hibiscus Surf School, Maunganui, T07-
575 3792, surfschool.co.nz. 2 hrs from $80.

Whakatane p85
Boat tours
Pee Jays, 15 Strand East, T07-308 9588,
T0800-733529, whiteisland.co.nz. The
best sea-based operator for the 5- to 6-hr
White Island volcano tour from $199.
Bookings essential.

East Cape to Gisborne p86
Rafting
Wet 'n' Wild Rafting, T07-348 3191,
wetnwild rafting.co.nz. Offers one of the
North Island's best wilderness rafting
expeditions, the multi-day trip down the
remote Motu River, from $995.

Transport

Bay of Plenty and East Cape p83
See Visiting Bay of Plenty and East Cape,
page 84.

Napier and Hawke's Bay

Napier is the principal town in Hawke's Bay and the largest on the east coast. It is a bright, dynamic place with the pleasant vibe of a Mediterranean coastal town. On the surface it enjoys the perfect relationship with nature: the rich fertile land and the warming sun making it the wine-producing capital of the North Island. However, it paid a heavy price in 1931 when an earthquake almost razed the town. Undeterred, the proud and determined people used this to their advantage and set about its rebuilding with an internationally recognized collection of art deco buildings thought to be amongst the finest in the world. Here, even the McDonalds is art deco.

Arriving in Napier

Getting around
Napier is on SH2, 321 km north of Wellington. The junction with SH5 and SH2 is about 6 km north of the town and from there it is 117 km to Taupo. Buses arrive and depart from the **Napier Travel Centre** ① *Munroe St, T06-835 2720, 0830-1700*. All major buses companies serve Hastings too. The i-SITE visitor centre acts as ticketing agents. **Gobus** ① *T06-835 8833, gobus.co.nz*, offers service in Napier and to Hastings and Havelock North.

Tourist information
Napier i-SITE visitor centre ① *100 Marine Parade, T06-834 1911, visit us.co.nz/hawkesbaynz. com, open daily 0900-1700.* **DoC** ① *59 Marine Parade, T06-834 3111, napier-ao@doc.govt.nz, Mon-Fri 0900-1615.* It has information about Cape Kidnappers Gannet Colony (plus tide times). **Hastings i-SITE visitor centre** ① *Westerman's Building, corner of Russell and Heretaunga streets, T06-873 5526, hawkesbaynz.com and hastings.co.nz, Mon-Fri 0830-1700, Sat-Sun 0900-1700.*

Napier

Marine Parade
Most of Napier's attractions lie along Marine Parade, which in itself creates an impressive perspective with its long promenade lined with Norfolk Pines and old wooden houses (the few that survived the earthquake). The Marine Parade Walkway starts at the northern end of Marine Parade. It features a number of art deco sculptures in a beachside garden setting and links several waterfront attractions that combine to create an almost European ambience.

First up, at the northern end heading south is the **Ocean Spa complex** ① *T06-835 8553, oceanspa.co.nz, Mon-Sat 0600-2200, Sun 0800-2200, $9.50, child $7.50, massage from $35.* It has hot pools, private spas, health and beauty therapies, and a café.

Almost immediately to the south of the spa complex gardens again predominate with a floral clock, the Tom Parker Fountain and **Pania of the Reef** statue. The fountain is just your average garden fountain by day but by night comes alive with a multi-coloured aquatic

Napier

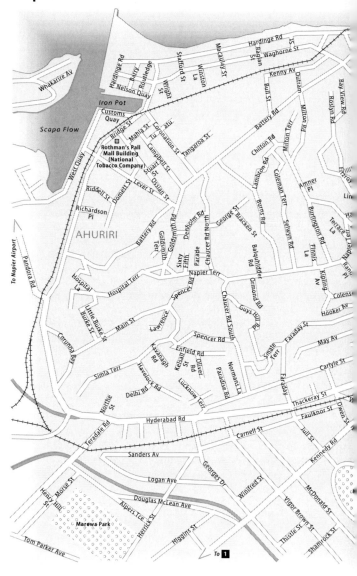

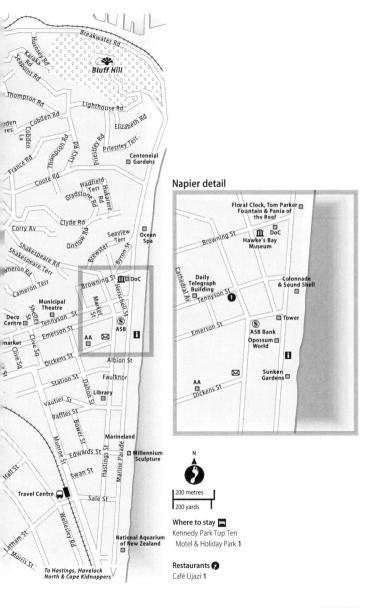

Napier detail

N

200 metres
200 yards

Where to stay
Kennedy Park Top Ten
  Motel & Holiday Park 1

Restaurants
Café Ujazi 1

Art deco architecture

The main attraction of Napier is its famous art deco and Spanish Mission architecture created after the devastating 1931 earthquake. On foot, the two central streets, Emerson and Tennyson, have many examples. On Emerson Street is the ASB Bank with its incorporated Maori designs and fine doorway, while on Tennyson Street the highlights are (from east to west) the Daily Telegraph Building, restored Municipal Theatre and the Deco Centre (art deco shop). Further afield is perhaps the most attractive building of all, the façade and entrance of the 1932 National Tobacco Company at the corner of Bridge and Ossian streets. Although somewhat distant from the town centre (in the port area of Westshore), it is worth the diversion. The building is even more impressive at night, when it is beautifully and imaginatively lit. Also worth seeing is the art deco McDonalds 'McDeco' in the suburb of Taradale (Gloucester St). For more comprehensive insight you can join a walking tour or pick up self-guided walking or driving leaflets from the i-SITE.

light show, while Pania is a small, attractive statue of a Maori maiden, with her legend o love described accordingly in a shower of the fountain's mist.

Heading south is the art deco Colonnade and Sound Shell. The Colonnade was once used for dancing and skating. Opposite the Sound Shell, which is occasionally used for open-air concerts, is the **Hawke's Bay Museum** ① *9 Herschell St, T06-8357781, hbmag. co.nz, closed at the time of research for redevelopment and due to reopen in 2013*, which offers a wide range of exhibits relating to the history and art of the region in modern surroundings. Nga Tukemata (The Awakening) presents the art and taonga of the local Maori and a rare presentation of evidence that dinosaurs once existed in New Zealand. Special attention is afforded to the earthquake of 1931. Relics from the rubble accompany audio-visual descriptions and touching memories of survivors.

Dominating the corner of Emerson Street and Marine Parade are the art deco Tower (The Dome) and the art deco Masonic Hotel.

Continuing south on Marine Parade you encounter the intriguing Millennium Sculpture created by local artist David Trubridge. The work is carefully lined up to where the sun rose at the dawning of the new millennium. Nearby The **National Aquarium of New Zealand** ① *T06-834 1404, national aquarium.co.nz, open daily 0900-1700, $17.90, child $8.90, behind-the-scenes tours $35.70, child $17.90, swim with the sharks from $75*, hosts an eclectic mix of native and non-native water and land creatures, from the enchanting seahorse to the iconic kiwi. The design of the building is quite clever, creating the impression that one is descending into the depths. Several remarkably toothy inhabitants will also have any unsuspecting herpetophobe breaking into a cold sweat.

Cape Kidnappers

Cape Kidnappers, the jagged white peninsula that marks the southern boundary of Hawke's Bay, is famous for its colony of gannets. These large, elegant seabirds have lots of attitude and, weighing in at about 2 kg with deadly 15-cm beaks designed to spear fish, they have every right to it. In the summer months, up to 15,000 gannets gather at Cape Kidnappers to breed, forming the biggest mainland colony in New Zealand, and one of the biggest in the world. Perhaps given their attitude and armoury, gannets are not particularly fearful of anything or anybody, which makes them very approachable, particularly when grouped together and guarding their own little breeding patch. The tourist visiting season runs from October to late April, with the best time to view being early November and late February.

There are two tours available to see the gannets. One operator negotiates the beach and the tides below the peninsula by tractor, the other goes overland (see page 94). The tractor-trailer affair is very entertaining for young and old and recommended. Provided the tides are right you can walk the 10 km to the colony yourself. The walk and beach tractor trip starts from the Clifton MotorCamp. 19 km southeast of Napier.

Hawke's Bay Vineyards

Given the climate and the soil in the Hawke's Bay area, it was inevitable that it would not take long for the first grapevine to be planted by the first Europeans settlers. Since then, the vines and the industry have boomed, making Hawke's Bay second only to Marlborough as the country's top wine-producing region. There are over 40 wineries in the area so unless you are a connoisseur, knowing which to visit can be a dilemma. Thankfully the free Hawke's Bay Winery Guide leaflet gives details of what each vineyard offers. Some like the **Sileni Estate** ⓘ *Maraekakaho Rd, Hastings, T06-879 8768, selini.co.nz.* have stunning architecture, others like **Craggy Range** ⓘ *253 Waimarama Rd, Havelock North, east of the village, T06-873 7126, craggyrange.com,* set in the shadow of Te Mata Peak enjoy admirable surroundings; some like the **Mission Estate** ⓘ *end of Avenue Rd, Taradale, T06-844 2259, missionestate.co.nz,* are very old, while others are particularly famous, more established, or have fine restaurants or cafés. Most offer sales and tastings. You can either embark on a tour according to your own choice and itinerary, or join a number of organized tours. If you know little about wines, and New Zealand wine in particular, an organized tour is advised (see page 94).

Hastings

Hastings is a lively, sprawling, mainly agricultural service centre 21 km south of Napier and, like Napier, it was devastated by the 1931 earthquake, with the loss of 93 lives. In rebuilding the town the architects echoed Napier's art deco and Spanish Mission styles, much of which can clearly be seen in the town centre. The two best examples are the **Westerman's Building** that now houses the i-SITE visitor centre on Russell Street and the refurbished HB Opera House on Hastings Street. During the summer the town is a blaze of colour for the annual Blossom Festival, when row upon row of hanging baskets line the streets providing a tourist attraction in itself and winning the town much praise around the country. Many remain year-round. Modern-day attractions in Hastings include the **Hawke's Bay Exhibition Centre** ⓘ *201 Eastbourne St, T06-876 2077, Mon-Fri 1000-1630, Sat-Sun 1100-1600, usually free depending on exhibitions,* which serves as the region's premier arts venue offering a varied programme of national and international touring exhibitions. Science and history also feature and there is an in-house café. If your visit to the town coincides with a Sunday the weekly **Farmers Market** ⓘ *Hawke's Bay Showgrounds, Kenilworth Rd, 0830-1230,* provides an ideal opportunity to meet locals and purchase fresh produce.

Havelock North and Te Mata Peak

Havelock North is a very pleasant little village nestled amongst vineyards and orchards towards the coast and in the shadow of the 399-m Te Mata Peak. The view from the summit of Te Mata on a clear day is a 'must-see' and it is easily reached by car via the village and Te Mata Peak Road. Weather permitting, it is also a popular spot for paragliding (see page 94).

Napier and Hawke's Bay listings

For hotel and restaurant price codes and other relevant information, see pages 9-14.

🛏 Where to stay

Napier *p89, map p90*
Motor parks
$$$-$ Kennedy Park Top Ten Motel and Holiday Park, Storkey St, T06-843 9126, kennedypark.co.nz. Popular, well-established and facilitated motor park and the closest to the town centre.

Havelock North *p93*
$$$$ Black Barn (Vineyard) Retreats, T06-877 7985, blackbarn.com. A superb selection of luxury lodge retreats or cottages, 8-2 bedroom, fully self contained and set in the heart of the vineyard.

🍴 Restaurants

Napier *p89, map p90*
$$$ Mission Estate, 198 Church Rd, Taradale, T06-845 9354, missionestate. co.nz. Daily for lunch and dinner, booking essential. This is the country's oldest winery and one of a number of vineyard restaurants. Has a solid reputation for quality contemporary cuisine with European influences. Outdoor seating available in summer.
$$-$ Café Ujazi, 28 Tennyson St, T06-835 1490. Daily from 0800. The local favourite in Napier. Good coffee, good vibe and a comprehensive blackboard menu. Vegetarian a speciality.

Havelock North *p93*
$$-$ Peak House Restaurant, Te Mata Peak Rd, T06-877 8663, peakhouse.co.nz. Wed-Mon 1000-1600. Perched 300 m up Te Mata Peak this is a great lunch or afternoon tea venue with a fantastic view.

✹ Festivals

Napier *p89, map p90*
Art Deco Weekend Held on the **3rd weekend of Feb**, Napier stages its annual Art Deco Weekend, a not-too-serious celebration of the art deco style. Locals dress in the deco style, classic cars grace the city streets and everyone enjoys the wining, dining, jazz, dancing, film, and theatre.

⬤ What to do

Napier *p89, map p90*
Tours
Gannet Beach Adventures, Clifton, T06-875 0898, T0800-426638, gannets.com. The oldest company and very entertaining. This 4-hr tour leaves daily (Oct-May) from Clifton Beach by tractor and allows about 1½ hrs with the gannets, from $38, child $23.

Havelock North *p93*
Paragliding
Airplay Paragliding, T06-845 1977/ 027-451 2886, airplay.co.nz. For those wishing to take to the sky over Te Mata Peak, paragliding flights and courses are available from $140.

Hastings *p93*
Tours
Grant Petherick Wine Tours ,T06-876 7467, flyfishingwinetours.co.nz. Quality, personable tours of the Hawke's Bay vineyards.

⬤ Transport

Napier and Hawke's Bay *p89*
See Arriving in Napier, page 89.

Taranaki and Wanganui

In many ways Taranaki is more mountain than region. The awesome 2518-m snow-capped volcanic cone of the same name seems to dominate everything and, even shrouded in mist, it is strangely omnipresent. Although many have enjoyed the volcano, it has also caused a number of deaths, and they say it is due for another eruption. However, whether you look at it with reverence or fear, it will always be the region's defining feature.

The largest town in the region is New Plymouth, a proud, prosperous and modern centre that lies in the shadow of Mount Taranaki on the northwest coast. Although a little bit out of the way, those who make the effort to visit the region will not be disappointed. As well as the superb scenery and range of activities on or around the mountain itself, the region boasts a fascinating history, fine parks, gardens, arts and crafts and a coastline internationally recognized for its excellent surfing.

Further south and east is the Wanganui Region, scythed almost in half by the Whanganui River, the longest navigable river in the North Island. Steeped in history, and supporting a rich watershed of remote hills adorned with native bush, much of the region is protected within the boundaries of the Whanganui National Park, a popular spot for kayakers and trampers, who leave civilization behind for days on end.

Visiting Taranaki and Wanganui

Getting around

New Plymouth is a little out of the way: 254 km from Hamilton on SH3 and 172 km from Wanganui, which is roughly halfway between Auckland and Wellington. Regional buses arrive and depart from the **New Plymouth Travel Centre** ① *19 Ariki St, T06-759 9039* The i-SITE visitor centre also handle bookings. The local bus company is **Taranaki Bus** ① *T0800-872287, trc.govt.nz*. For mountain transport contact **Taranaki Tours** ① *T06-757 9888, taranakitours.com*.

Tourist information

New Plymouth i-SITE visitor centre ① *Puke Ariki Museum and Library, near the waterfront, 65 St Aubyn St, T06-759 6060, newplymouthnz.com or taranaki.co.nz, Mon, Tue, Thu, Fri 0900-1800, Wed 0900-2100, Sat-Sun 0900-1700*. **DoC** ① *55A Rimu St, New Plymouth, T06-759 0350, wanganuiconservancy@doc.govt.nz*, for detailed Egmont National Park information **Wanganui i-SITE visitor centre** ① *101 Guyton St, T06-3490508, wanganuinz.com, destinationwanganui.com, rivernz.com, Mon-Fri 0830-1700, Sat-Sun 0900-1500*.

New Plymouth

Based on resources of rich agricultural land and natural gas and oil supplies, lively New Plymouth enjoys considerable prosperity and is the main service town and population base of the Taranaki Region. The town, and the entire district, is dominated by the mountain, which seems to dictate the general mood, like some huge meteorological barometer. On a clear day, when the mountain radiates, its sheer size and stature are mirrored proudly in the town and the region. But, when shrouded in mist and rain, the area feels dull and somber. As well as being a fine base from which to explore the recreational delights on and around the mountain and the region as a whole, New Plymouth itself has an excellent art gallery, some interesting historic buildings and a fine marine and public park.

The rather flash **Taranaki Museum and Library (Puke Ariki)** ① *Egmont St, T06-759 6060, pukeariki.com, Mon, Tue, Thu, Fri 0900-1800, Wed 0900-2100, Sat/Sun 0900-1700, free, temporary exhibitions $6*, houses an interesting collection of Maori artifacts and displays, mixed with the usual pioneer exhibits and wildlife specimens. Obviously the great mountain features heavily and this is an opportunity to learn of its importance to the region, if not its power.

One of the town's most celebrated institutions is the **Govett-Brewster Gallery** ① *corner of Queen and King streets, T06-759 6060, govettbrewster.com, daily 1000-1700, free*. The interior is on three levels and looks very modern, befitting its reputation as the premier contemporary art gallery in the country. The gallery doyen is Len Lye, a poet, writer and multimedia artist who specialized in pioneering animation work in the 1930s. His best-known work is the **Wind Wand** on the waterfront near the museum. Created for the millennium celebrations it is a 45-m, 900-kg kinetic sculpture that is designed to sway gently in the breeze. The bulb at the end is lit at night to enhance this effect. New Plymouth is famous for its extensive and feature-filled parks, the oldest and finest of which are **Pukekura Park** and **Brooklands Park**, which merge together. On the southern edge of the city near the ugly towers of the power station and the port is the **Sugar Loaf Island Marine Park** with its eroded, volcanic rock islands. It is home to fur seals and a variety of nesting seabirds. Boat trips to visit the park and view the wildlife are available. The shoreline of the park is part of an interesting 7-km Coastal Walkway, the highlight of which is the climb up **Paritutu Rock**.

Around New Plymouth

Carrington Road (off Victoria Rd) heads southwest out of New Plymouth towards the mountain. It has a number of sights including **The Pukeiti Rhododendron Trust Gardens** ① *2290 Carrington Rd, T06-752 4141, daily 0900-1700, winter 1000-1500, $15, $10 in winter*. This is a 4-sq-km garden surrounded by bush that is world-renowned for its beautiful displays of 'rhodies' and azaleas, which are best viewed in the spring/summer and especially during the Rhododendron Festival in late October. There is a restaurant, and a shop selling plants and souvenirs.

If you continue on Carrington Road you will join the network of roads that surround the mountain. There is a fine walk and views of the mountain on the Stony River and Blue Rata reserves.

There is something you simply must do on your visit to New Plymouth (weather permitting) and that is to soak up the beauty and serenity of **Lake Mangamahoe**. Just 10 km southeast on SH3, this scenic reserve is one of the very best places where you can see a reflection of the mighty mountain on water. After enjoying the lake itself, head to the road end and take the right hand track up the steps to the lookout point. From here at sunset, or anytime when the mountain is clear, the view is magnificent.

If you fancy doing the 175-km trip around the mountain, it involves at least a full day via the Surf Highway 45 and SH3. But on a clear day the mountain will be good company throughout, and there are a number of interesting places to see and visit on the way including the **Cape Egmont Lighthouse**, about 3 km down Cape Road. Although the lighthouse is closed to visitors it is still of interest. Back on SH45, you can enjoy the scenery or explore the many side roads until you reach Opunake and Manaia, which is the place to leave SH45 if you want to get a bit more intimate with the mountain at **Dawson Falls**. You can also stay there if you wish to attempt the summit walk and there is a **DoC visitors centre** ① *Manaia Rd, Kaponga, T06-7560990*, to obtain the detail. At Dawson Falls there are also some good short-walk options.

Mount Egmont (Taranaki) National Park

Weather permitting, no trip to Taranaki would be complete without getting close to the mountain. At 2518 m, Mount Taranaki is a classically shaped, dormant volcano formed by the numerous eruptions of the last 12,000 years. The most recent happened 350 years ago and they say she is now overdue, with the potential to go off at any time. But don't worry these days there would be plenty of warning.

The main access points to the park and the mountain are at North Egmont (Egmont visitor information centre), Stratford (East Egmont) and Manaia (Dawson Falls). East Egmont is accessed via Pembroke Road, which heads 18 km towards the mountain from Stratford. Dawson Falls is at the end of Upper Manaia Road, via Kaponga on the southern slopes of the mountain, 24 km from Stratford. If you do not have your own transport, **Taranaki Tours** ① *Manaia Rd, Kaponga, T06-7560990 T06-757 9888, taranakitours.com*, offer shuttle services to the mountain from New Plymouth (particularly north Egmont), from $55 return.

Before attempting any major walks on the mountain you should read all the relevant information. The i-SITE visitor centre in New Plymouth can provide basic information, while the DoC office (both in town and on the mountain) can fill in the detail with walking information, maps and weather forecasts.

The 140-km of walks take from 30 minutes to four days and are well maintained. The tracks vary in difficulty, but all are easily accessible from the main access points and information centres above. The forest and vegetation is called 'goblin forest' (due to its miniature hobbit-style appearance as the altitude increases) and the entire mountain is drained by myriad babbling streams.

Wanganui and the Whanganui River National Park

Wanganui lies at the mouth of the Whanganui River roughly halfway between New Plymouth and Wellington.

Proud of its river and once a bustling port, Wanganui is now principally an agricultural service town and the southern gateway to the Whanganui River National Park. The town boasts a rich heritage and retains some fine buildings as well as a reputable museum and many parks and gardens. In summer the main street is ablaze with a thousand hanging baskets of flowers and throughout the year the restored steamboat **Waimarie** plies the great river, reminding both locals and visitors of days gone by.

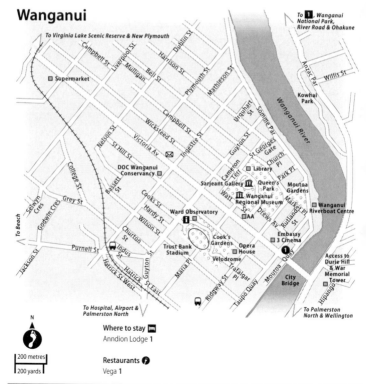

Wanganui

Where to stay 🛏
Anndion Lodge 1

Restaurants 🍴
Vega 1

From Wanganui the river it begins its 290-km journey inland, carving its way through some of the most remote and inaccessible country in the North Island. Negotiable by waka (canoe) and steamboat for much of its length, the region is rich in both Maori and European history, from the first days of early exploration and settlement through to the river's renaissance as a tourist and recreational attraction. Although the park is hard to access (which is undoubtedly part of its charm), there is the opportunity to explore the historical sites of the river and enjoy its atmosphere. You can do this, in part on its banks by road and walking tracks, or on the river itself by jet boat or kayak.

Taranaki and Wanganui listings

For hotel and restaurant price codes and other relevant information, see pages 9-14.

☺ Where to stay

New Plymouth *p96*
$$$ The Nice Hotel, 71 Brougham St, T06-758 6423, nicehotel.co.nz. A small luxury boutique hotel well placed for the town centre and all amenities. Each of the 8 rooms is themed according to its outlook and reflects the town's history or contribution to the arts. As well as stylish design, the rooms offer all the comforts. The popular restaurant is relaxed.

Motor parks
$$-$ Egmont Eco Leisure Park, 12 Clawton St, T06-753 5720, egmont. co.nz. Set in native bush with lodge, cabins powered and tent sites, fully equipped camp kitchen. A short walk from the town centre.

Wanganui *p98, map p98*
$$-$ Anndion Lodge, 2 km from the centre, 143 Anzac Parade, T06-343 3593, anndionlodge.co.nz. Top-quality option pitched between a modern backpacker hostel and a motel. Offers modern and tidy riverside accommodation, with rooms ranging from super-king to dorms at reasonable prices. Well facilitated with spa, internet, off-street parking.

❼ Restaurants

New Plymouth *p96*
$$$ Andre L'Escargot, 37-43 Brougham St, T06-758 4812. Mon-Sat from 1700. This is long-established regional favourite offering award-winning, fine French-style cuisine in a congenial setting. Now offers affordable Bistro Chic set menus for around $50.

Wanganui *p98, map p98*
$$$-$$ Vega Restaurant, 49 Taupo Quay, T06-349 0078. Lunch Tue-Sun, daily for dinner. Classy establishment set in a converted warehouse near the river. It has earned a reputation as the city's finest, especially for seafood. Excellent wine list.

❸ Transport

Taranaki and Wanganui *p95*
See Visiting Taranaki and Wanganui, page 96.

Contents

Wellington & around

Wellington

If you can defy that inevitable eagerness to board the ferry and don't mind dodging the odd suit, you certainly won't regret it. Wellington offers a wealth of things to see and do from the impressive icons of Te Papa (Museum of New Zealand) and the incongruous Beehive, to cable-car rides and kiwi spotting. Also, with more restaurants per capita than just about any city on earth, it is the ideal place to sample some of the best of Australasia's Pacific Rim cuisine.

Arriving in Wellington

Getting there

The scenic 85-km journey across Cook Strait takes three hours. There are currently two services: the **Interislander** ① *T0800-802802/04-4983302, interislander.co.nz*, and the smaller of the two companies **Bluebridge** ① *T0800-844844/T04-4716188, bluebridgeco.nz*

The latter has older vessels, tend to be cheaper and is the best choice if you are looking for character and a more traditional ferry experience. In adverse weather conditions the crossing can be a bit of an ordeal. Sailings will be cancelled if conditions are considered too dangerous, but this is rare. Advance booking in advance is advised at all times, but especially in December/January. Most major i-SITES and travel agents can organize bookings and tickets. A free shuttle bus to the Interislander terminal (2 km) is available from the Wellington railway station (Platform 9), 30 minutes before each scheduled ferry departure.

Various day/limited-excursion, family and group fares and standard discounted fares are available but must be booked in advance and are subject to availability. Like most travel bookings these days the internet will secure the best deals. At peak periods (particularly December/January) discounts are rarely available. Fares for passengers range from a standard vehicle with two passengers from about $273 one-way, a motor home with two passengers $365 and two passengers no vehicle $65 per person.

Wellington is 658 km from Auckland. The principal route is via SH1. Martinborough is 65 km via SH2, the principal route to the Wairarapa and the east coast. **Wellington airport** ① *Miramar, 6 km south of the centre, T04-3855100, wellingtonairport.co.nz*, has regular services to all the main domestic centres. The taxi fare into town is about $35. Shuttle buses can be shared for about $15, T0800-748885. The Airport Flyer is an express bus service that runs from the airport to the centre of Wellington every 15 minutes, $8. For $12 the 'StarPass' will give you unlimited travel for one day on Airport Flyer, Valley Flyer & GO Wellington services.

Regional buses arrive and depart from the **train station** ① *Bunny St, Intercity, T04-385 0520*. The train station is next to the quay on Bunny Street.

Tourist information

Wellington i-SITE visitor centre ① *corner of Wakefield and Victoria streets, T04-802 4860, wellingtonnz.com, Mon-Fri 0830-1800, Sat-Sun 0930-1700.* **Palmerston North and Destination Manawatu i-SITE visitor centre** ① *The Square, T06-350 1922, manawatunz. co.nz, daily 0900-1700.* **Martinborough i-SITE visitor centre** ① *18 Kitchener St, Martinborough, Wairarapa, T06-306 9043, wairarapanz.com, daily 0900-1600.*

Places in Wellington

Mount Victoria Lookout

Most of Wellington's major attractions are within walking distance or a short bus ride from each other. An ideal spot to get your bearings is the 196-m Mount Victoria Lookout southeast from the city centre. The view is spectacular at sunrise and after dark. Although from a distance the wooded sides of the mount hardly seem in character with the film trilogy *Lord of the Rings* it proved both a convenient and aesthetically suitable location for several scenes depicting The Shire in the first film, the Fellowship of the Ring.

Thorndon and the Parliamentary District

The suburb of Thorndon, to which the Parliamentary District essentially belongs, is the oldest and most historic in Wellington.

The Parliamentary District is centered on and around Bowen Street, in the Lambton Quarter just west of the rather grand-looking railway station. You will be immediately struck by the rather odd and aptly named **Beehive**, which houses the various government offices full of workers, the odd swarm of killers and, until recently, the Queen bee herself – Helen Clarke – one of the nation's longest-serving Prime Ministers. Designed by British architect Sir Basil Spence, and built in 1980, the honeyless hive is either loved or hated. **Parliament's visitor centre** ① *T04-817 9503, parliament.nz,* is in the ground floor foyer of the Beehive. Far more aesthetically pleasing is the 1922 **Old Parliament House** ① *Mon-Fri 0900-1700, Sat 0930-1600, Sun 1130-1600; regular tours are available and you can also see parliament in session.* While in the vicinity of Parliament House take a peek or stop for lunch in the **Backbencher Pub**, across the road on Molesworth Street facing the High Court. Adorning the walls are some superb cartoons and Spitting Image-style dummies of past and present prime ministers.

Just a short stroll from the Backbencher Pub on Lambton Quay is the historic **Old Government Buildings** built in 1876 to house the Crown Ministers and public servants of the day. The building was designed to look like stone but actually constructed of wood and is the second largest wooden building in the world (the largest being the Todaiji Temple in Nara City, Japan). It now houses the Victoria University's Law Faculty.

Also in the Parliamentary District is the **National Library Gallery** ① *5 Molesworth St, T04-474 3000, Mon-Fri 0900-1700, Sat 0900-1300,* with its impressive collection of research books, colonial photographs and in-house gallery. It also has a shop and a café. **The Archives New Zealand** ① *10 Mulgrave St, Thorndon, T04-499 5595, archives.govt.nz, Mon-Fri 0900-1700, Sat 0900-1300, free,* have within its hallowed walls a number of important historical documents including the original and controversial Treaty of Waitangi.

Also of historical and literary note in Thorndon is the birthplace of **Katherine Mansfield** ① *25 Tinakori Rd, T06-473 7268, katherinemansfield.com, Tue-Sun 1000-1600, $8.* Mansfield is generally hailed as New Zealand's most famous writer. The house and gardens have been faithfully restored and there is an interesting video portrait of the writer.

Wellington

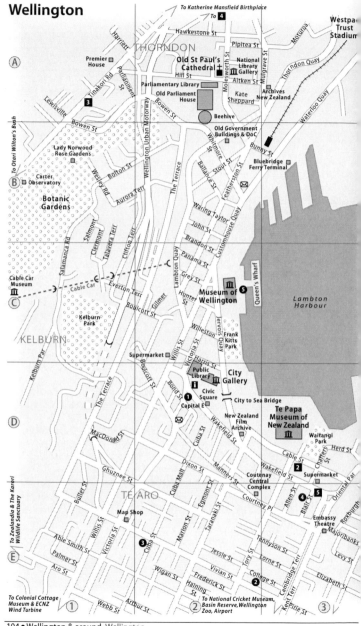

To Katherine Mansfield Birthplace
To **4**

Westpac Trust Stadium

Hawkestone St

THORNDON

Pipitea St

Moturoa

A Premier House

Old St Paul's Cathedral

National Library Gallery

Mulgrave St

Thorndon Quay

Harriett

Parliament St

Hill St

Molesworth St

Aitken St

Parliamentary Library

3 Tinakori Rd

Old Parliament House

Kate Sheppard

Archives New Zealand

Lewisville

Beehive

Waterloo Quay

Bowen St

Bowen St

Old Government Buildings & DoC

Bunny St

B Lady Norwood Rose Gardens

Bolton St

Whitmore St

Bluebridge Ferry Terminal

Carter Observatory

Wesley Rd

The Terrace

Stout St

Featherston St

Botanic Gardens

Aurora Terr

Ballance St

Waring Taylor Quay

Customhouse Quay

John St

Salmont

Talavera Terr

Brandon St

Clermont

Panama St

Clifton Terr

Lambton Quay

Grey St

Cable Car Museum

Cable Car

Everton Terr

Hunter St

Museum of Wellington **5**

Queen's Wharf

Lambton Harbour

C Gilmer

Boulcott St

KELBURN

Kelburn Park

Jervois Quay

Kelburn Par

Willeston St

Frank Kitts Park

The Terrace

Boulcott St

Supermarket

Willis St

Victoria St

Harris St

Public Library

City Gallery

City to Sea Bridge

1 Civic Square

Capital E

D MacDonald St

Bond St

Wakefield St

New Zealand Film Archive

Te Papa Museum of New Zealand

Waitangi Park

Cable St

Herd St

Ghuznee St

Dixon St

Manners St

Cuba St

Wakefield St

2 Chaffers St

Supermarket

To Zealandia & The Karori Wildlife Sanctuary

Butler St

Map Shop

Egmont St

Courtenay Central Complex

Allen St

4 **5**

Oriental Par

TE ARO

Marion St

Taranaki St

Courtenay Pl

Blair St

Roxburgh

E Able Smith St

Willis St

Victoria St

Cuba St **3**

Embassy Theatre

Majoribanks

Palmer St

Wigan St

Marton St

Tory St

Tennyson St

Cambridge Terr

Levy St

Aro St

Arthur St

Webb St

Frederick St

Haining St

Vivian St

Jessie St

Lorne St

Cottage St **2**

Ken Terr

Elizabeth St

To Colonial Cottage Museum & ECNZ Wind Turbine

1

2 To National Cricket Museum, Basin Reserve, Wellington Zoo, Airport

Pirie St

3

Civic Square and the waterfront

Civic Square, just behind the i-SITE visitor centre has some interesting architectural features and is often used for outdoor events. The redeveloped **City Gallery** ⓘ *T04-8013021, citygallery.org.nz, daily 1000-1700, free*, is located here and given Wellington is considered the artistic heart of the nation, the gallery strives (successfully it would seem) to present a regular programme of the very best of contemporary visual arts.

From Civic Square it is a short walk across the very arty **City to Sea Bridge**, which connects the square with the waterfront. The bridge sprouts a number of interesting sculptures that celebrate the arrival of the Maori in New Zealand.

The waterfront has become a major focus in the city for its museums, aesthetics and recreational activities.

The temptation is to head south and to lose oneself in the impressive Te Papa Museum of New Zealand, but it is worth heading north first, past Frank Kitts Park and the wharf to the **Museum of Wellington City and Sea** ⓘ *T04-472 8904, museumofwellington.co.nz, daily 1000-1700, free*.

Being in such close proximity to Te Papa, you might think its attempts to compete and woo visitors was an exercise in futility, but this museum is actually superb and, in its own way, competes favourably with Te Papa. As the name suggests, the emphasis is on local history, with a particular maritime bent. Of note are the Wahine Ferry Disaster Gallery and the state-of-the-art holographic display on Maori legends. The Wahine was a passenger ferry that came to grief at the harbour entrance in 1968 with the loss of 51 lives.

Te Papa Museum of New Zealand
ⓘ *55 Cable St, T04-3817111, tepapa.govt. nz. Daily 1000-1800, Thu 1000-2100, free, (around $15 for temporary exhibitions). Allow at least half a day at the museum. 1-hr 'Introducing Te Papa Tours' available Nov-Apr*

daily on the hour 1000-1500, $14; Apr-Oct 1015 and 1400. Specialist tours (including a Maori Experience Tour) are available at a cost.

To the south of Civic Square and gracing the harbour's eastern bank is the unmistakable Te Papa Museum of New Zealand – Wellington's biggest tourist attraction. As if the exterior was not enough, the interior is also mind-bending. Heavily publicised Te Papa has faithfully represented the nation's heritage since 1998, at an initial cost of $317 million. Since then over twice the population of the nation itself (9.3 million) have passed through its doors and few have been disappointed.

In Te Papa they say there is something for everybody and this does seem to hold true. As expected, there is a heavy emphasis on Maori heritage, taonga (treasures) and biculturalism, mixed with the inevitable early settler material, contemporary displays of all things Kiwi and 'Toi Te Papa' – an exhibition of 130 New Zealand artworks.

More recently it was the turn of the natural history section to grab the headlines with the arrival and display of the world's largest specimen of colossal squid. The half-ton, 10-m long specimen arrived at the museum in March 2007, after being captured in New Zealand waters a month before.

Given entry to the museum is free, it is a good idea to have an initial quick recce and return later for a more in-depth investigation to avoid the almost inevitable information overload.

There is an excellent shop on the ground floor, but the café is less than impressive.

Botanic Gardens, Cable Car and Cable Car Museum

ⓘ *The main entrance is on Glenmore St in Thorndon, T04-499 1400, wellington.govt.nz. Gardens open dawn till dusk, free. Cable car, T04-472 2199, runs every 10 mins, Mon-Fri 0700-2200, Sat-Sun 0830-2200, $5, child $2 return.*

Wellington's Botanic Gardens are really quite magnificent and by far the best way to visit them is via the Cable Car at 280 Lambton Quay. First built in 1902 and now a tourist attraction in itself, the almost completely subterranean single line has cables that haul the two lovely red carriages up and down, with four stops on the way. When your carriage glides in quietly to the summit (Kelburn) station you step out into the gardens and are immediately rewarded with a fine view across the city. **The Cable Car Museum** ⓘ *T04-475 3578, cablecarmuseum.co.nz, daily 0930-1730, free*, is also located at the summit and houses some lovingly restored cars and interpretive displays.

Beyond the museum there are 26 ha of specialist gardens, radiant flowerbeds, foreign trees and native bush to explore. Not surprisingly one of the most popular spots is the **Lady Norwood Rose Garden** where you can muse upon the names and fragrances of more than 300 varieties form a budding pink 'Little Willy' to the rather disheveled 'Nancy Reagan'.

The gardens also play host to the recently redeveloped **Carter Observatory** ⓘ *T04-472 8167, carterobservatory.org*. It has static displays, planetarium shows and audio-visuals.

You can also find a very fragrant and relaxing café next to the **rose gardens** ⓘ *Mon-Fri 1100-1500, Sat-Sun 1000-1600.*

Zelandia and The Karori Wildlife Sanctuary

ⓘ *Waiapu Rd, Karori, T04-920 9200, visitzealandia.com. Daily 1000-1700, from $18.50, child $9*

The Karori Wildlife Sanctuary is a great conservation success story and a tribute to an army of devoted volunteers. In 1994 an area of 250 ha was set aside and protected with a predator-proof fence. This was of course a challenge and an expensive one at that, but was done to hopefully repeat the efficacy of New Zealands offshore islands. Now, with the eradication of non-native pest species within the boundary of the fence, the benefits for both native flora and fauna are plain to see. Reintroduced species like kaka (native parrot) and the 'living fossil' tuatara are making a solid comeback and birdsong is returning to native bush that once lay silent. The sanctuary has over 30 km of bush walks to explore its many features from the lake to specialist feeding stations. A new visitor centre is currently under construction with state-of-the-art interactive exhibitions that tell the story of New Zealand's unique natural history from the day before humans arrived through to the groundbreaking conservation techniques of today. It will also house a shop and café. There are guided tours daily and also at night to view or hear nocturnal wildlife, including the resident kiwi, from $60, child $30, pick-ups from the i-SITE.

Around Wellington

Oriental Bay to Owhiro and the Weta Cave

If you have your own vehicle there is a very pleasant drive around the Miramar peninsula with its pleasant bay suburbs and coastal scenery.

Start from Oriental Bay and follow the road round to the airport then take Shelley Bay Road around the next headland to Palmer Head and Scorching Bay on the edge of Seatoun. There are some good beaches in the area, suitable for sunbathing and swimming. Note this is also the home of little blue penguins that come ashore to roost at night, often under the old waterside houses. While in Miramar it is worth calling in at the **Weta Cave** ① *corner of Camperdown Rd and Weka St, Miramar, T04-380 9361, wetanz.com/cave, open daily 0900-1730, free*. Weta Workshops was founded in part by Peter Jackson and was the group of incredibly talented creative's responsible for the characters, props and special effects for films like *Lord of the Rings*, *King Kong* and most recently *The Hobbit*. The Weta Cave is a small museum that takes a detailed look at the Weta Workshops phenomenon including screened interviews with its founders and artists. There are also some of the famous – or infamous – characters, props and displays from the movies and a shop selling Weta-designed clothing, jewellery and mementos.

On the way back to the city from Owhiro Bay west of the airport, try to take in the eclectic metal and junk creations of **Carl Gifford's Stonewall Co** ① *287 Happy Valley Rd, T04-971 8618, stonewallco.net.nz*. Call at the house for sales and permission to view at close hand.

There is also a New Zealand fur seal colony at Red Rocks which is accessed via the quarry track at the western end of Owhiro Bay (4 km), but if you are short of time, don't worry you will see plenty more on the shores of the South Island or Cape Palliser.

Wellington listings

For hotel and restaurant price codes and other relevant information, see pages 9-14.

⊙ Where to stay

Wellington *p102, map p104*
$$$$-$$$ Museum Hotel-Hotel De Wheels, 90 Cable St, T04-802 8900, museumhotel.co.nz. A modern boutique establishment ideally located across the road from Te Papa and in the heart of the café, bar and restaurant areas. It oozes class and along with all the standard facilities also has fully self-serviced luxury apartments.
$$$-$$ The Shepherds Arms Hotel, 285 Tinakori Rd, Thorndon, T04-472 1320, T0800-393782, shepherds.co.nz. Conveniently located historic hotel within walking distance from the city and botanical gardens, offering a wide range of boutique accommodation from singles or doubles to King Suite with spa and 4-poster. There is also a good restaurant and bar with a open fire and parking.
$$-$ Wellington YHA, 292 Wakefield St, T04-801 7280, yha.org.nz. Deservingly popular with a wide range of rooms (some with en suite bathrooms and TV, excellent facilities and helpful friendly staff. All this just a stone's throw from Courtenay Quarter's cafés and restaurants, a major supermarket and Te Papa. The only drawback is the lack of off-street parking.

Self-catering
$$$ Austinvilla B&B, 11 Austin St, Mt Victoria, T04-385 8334, austinvilla.co.nz. Set in a villa on the slopes of Mt Victoria and with views across to the city this is a great self-contained B&B option. 2 separate fully self-contained units with private entrance, within walking distance of Courtenay Place.

Motor parks
There are no motor parks in Wellington itself. The best and nearest are in Lower Hutt. You might also like to consider the motor park at Paekakariki.
$$$-$ Top-Ten Hutt Park Holiday Park, 95 Hutt Park Rd, Lower Hutt, T04-568 5913, huttpark.co.nz. Around 20 mins from the city centre. Standard Top Ten facilities with a full range of accommodation options, from 2-bedroom motel-style units, to non-powered campsites. Camp kitchen, spa and internet.
$$-$ Paekakariki Holiday Park, 180 Wellington Rd, T04-292 8292, paekakarikiholidaypark.co.nz. Above-average facilities and good location close to the beach and adjacent to Queen Elizabeth Park. 40 mins to ferry outside rush hour.

⊙ Restaurants

Wellington *p102, map p104*
Wellington prides itself on its thriving café and restaurant scene. The Courtenay Quarter is where most are located with a number of pubs offering fine, reliable and mainly international or Pacific Rim cuisine. Cuba Street has numerous inexpensive restaurants, funky cafés and takeaways, while Queen's Wharf is a favourite haunt at lunchtime.
$$$ Logan Brown, 192 Cuba St, T04-801 5114, loganbrown.co.nz. Lunch Mon-Fri, dinner daily. A well-established, multi award-winning establishment, offering international cuisine in the old historic and spacious banking chambers.
$$$ Shed 5, Queen's Wharf, T04-499 9069, shed5.co.nz. Daily from 1100. A fine evening venue, but popular during the day and at weekends. The menu is mainly seafood or Mediterranean.
$$ Café Lido, opposite the i-SITE, T04-4996666. Mon 0730-1500, Tue-Fri 0730-late, Sat-Sun 0730-late. One of the most popular in the city and always busy especially for breakfast. A fine place to mix with Wellingtonians and watch the world go by.

\$\$ Café L'Affare, 27 College St, T04-385
9748. Mon-Fri 0700-1630, Sat 0800-1600.
Well worth the extra walk. It is a thriving
coffee business as well as an excellent café,
full of atmosphere. As you might expect,
the coffee (and even the smell of the place)
is sublime.

\$\$ Kai, 21 Majoribanks St, T04-801 5006.
Mon-Sat from 1730. A truly Maori eating
experience and it doesn't come much
better than this. Small and friendly, with
a range of traditional Maori dishes from
kumara pies (Pacific sweet potato) to kuku
(steamed green-lipped mussels) all for a
reasonable price.

\$\$ Monsoon Poon, 12 Blair St, T04-803
3555. Mon-Thu 1100-2300, Fri 1100-2400,
Sat 1700-2400, Sun 1700-until the chefs
get tired. Considered the pick of the Asian
restaurants, offering a wide range of dishes
from Thai to Vietnamese. The chefs do their
thing in full view of the spacious dining
floor. Lively bar, great atmosphere.

☻ Entertainment

Wellington p102, map p104
Although Aucklanders would disagree,
Wellington probably has the edge when
it comes to a good night out. As well as a
large number of pubs and clubs, there are
numerous venues including large concert
halls such as the **Michael Fowler Centre**,
offering rock and classical, and noted
theatres such as the **Westpac St James** and
Circa offering contemporary drama, dance
and comedy.

For listings ask at the VIC or check the
daily newspaper *The Dominion Post* or the
tourist paper *Capital Times*. Useful websites
are: feelinggreat.co.nz or wellington
nz.com. Tickets for major events can be
bought from **Ticketek**, Michael Fowler
Centre, 111 Wakefield St, T04-384 3840,
ticket ek.co.nz, i-SITE sometimes offers
discounts on theatre tickets.

Theatre
The Embassy Theatre, 10 Kent Terr, at the
bottom of Courtenay Pl, T04-384 7657,
deluxe.co.nz. This deserves special mention
due to its giant screen (one of the largest in
the southern hemisphere). It was also used
to host the premieres of Kiwi director Peter
Jackson's *Lord of the Rings* trilogy.

☻ Festivals

Wellington p102, map p104
Feb/Mar International Rugby Sevens
Tournament, T04-389 0020, nzisevens.co.nz.
The world's best rugby sevens teams run
around like loonies at the Westpac Stadium.
New Zealand International Arts Festival,
T04-473 0149, nzfestival.nzpost.co.nz.
This is a biennial event (next in 2014) and
Wellington's most celebrated. It lasts for
three weeks and is currently the country's
largest cultural event with a rich and varied
pageant of music performers, drama, street
theatre, traditional Maori dance, modern
dance and visual arts.
Sep World of Wearable Art Awards,
T03-548 9299, worldofwearableart.com.
A unique Kiwi arts affair that has grown
from strength to strength from humble
beginnings in the country's arts capital,
Nelson. This is your once in a lifetime
chance to see models dress as a banana,
or a boat, or in something made of copious
sticky back plastic and toilet roll holders.
Anything is possible and it is incredibly
creative. Even former PM Helen Clarke once
hit the catwalk donned in a fetching kind
of paua shell little number – sort of.

◯ Shopping

Wellington p102, map p104
Wellington is a fine city for shopaholics.
The main shopping areas are Lambton
Quay, Willis, Cuba and Courtenay streets. For
quality souvenirs try the shop at Te Papa.

As you might expect, Cuba St's wide
variety of cafés and restaurants are echoed

in the nature of its shops. Whether it is 1970s clothing, second-hand books, utter kitsch, a pair of skin-tight pink plastic pants or an erotic device (batteries not included), this is where to go. It is always good fun to muse even if you do not indulge yourself.

Along Lambton Quay, nicknamed The Golden Mile, the retail highlights are the elegant boutique shops of the Old Bank and the unfortunately named Kirkcaldie and Stains, Wellington's answer to Harrods.

🚌 What to do

Wellington *p102, map p104*
Tours
Flat Earth Tours, T04-9775805, T0800-775805, flatearth.co.nz. An excellent tour company offering an exciting range of tours with the quintessential 'capital' edge, from a Wild Wellington Tour that focuses on local native wildlife; a Maori Treasures Tour that offers demonstrations of art and crafts (with an opportunity to create an artwork of your own); a Classic Wine Tour to the Wairarapa and of course the inevitable *Lord of the Rings* tour. Other options include sightseeing and a city arts tour. Tours are half or full-day and start from around $159.
Zest, T04-4791778, zestfoodtours.co.nz. This operator offers a package for small groups of self-confessed gourmands, whipping up the ingredients of local knowledge and fascinating ventures behind the scenes to create a fine tour experience. Walking option 0930-1330, from $169.

🚉 Transport

Wellington *p102, map p104*
Wellington offers air, train and nationwide bus services. See also Arriving in Wellington page 102.

Bus
Wellington bus services are operated by Metlink, T0800-801700, metlink.org.nz.

Train
TranzScenic operates the daily 'Overlander' service from Auckland, T0800-872467/04-495 0775, tranzscenic.co.nz. TranzMetro, T0800-801700, tranzmetro.co.nz, offers regular daily services from the Wairarapa including Martinborough (bus link) and Masterton direct.

ⓘ Directory

Wellington *p102, map p104*
ATM All the major banks with ATMs are represented in the CBD especially along Willis St and Lambton Quay. **Hospital** Wellington Hospital, Riddiford St, T04-385 5999. **Pharmacy** Medical Centre Building, 729 High St, T04-939 6777. Corner Victoria and Harris streets, T04-3812000.

Kapiti Coast and Palmerston North

Just north of Wellington, SH1 slices its way through the hills of a major fault-line and passes the rather dull town of Porirua before joining the picturesque Kapiti coastline. For the next 30 km the small coast and inland settlements of Paekakariki, Waikanae and Otaki are shadowed by Kapiti Island on one side and the Tararua Forest Park on the other. Kapiti Island is well worth a visit while Paekakariki, Paraparaumu and Waikanae offer a number of interesting local sights and activities. Otaki is the principal access point to the Tararua Forest Park.

Paraparaumu and Waikanae

Paraparaumu is the principal township on the Kapiti Coast and has close ties with Wellington both as commuter town and as a seaside resort popular during the summer months. There are two main beaches, Raumati to the south and Paraparaumu Beach to the north. All the usual facilities are here and the town also serves as the gateway to Kapiti Island. A little further north on SH1 is the small satellite town of Waikanae, which also prides itself on its fine beach. Paraparaumu's main claim to fame came in 2001 when Tiger Woods was lured with a rather attractive $2 million to play at the New Zealand Open golf challenge on its world-class golf course, T04-902 8200.

Kapiti Island

Kapiti Island is a very special place; not only is it a delight to visit but it's like going back in time to when New Zealand was an unspoiled paradise. Lying 5 km offshore from Paraparaumu, it is 10 km long, 2 km wide and is now one of the most important reserves in the country protected and nurtured by DoC. It took a huge budget and six years of hunting and poisoning in the 1980s to rid the island of 22,500 possums, while further exhaustive helicopter poison drops in the 1990s have been successful in keeping rats at bay. After numerous plant and animal re-introductions, the results are the first signs of regeneration and hints of what once was. Here you are in nature's territory – not human. You can walk on a number of well-kept tracks through proper New Zealand bush. Inquisitive birds like robin, saddleback and stitchbird flit about your head, while weka and takahe poke about for insects disturbed by your feet. At night you can hear kiwi, or share the coastal path with little blue penguins that do not run in fear, but merely stick their heads in the grass and croak at you with their little white bottoms sticking in the air. And at dawn, if you are very lucky, you can hear one of the most beautiful bird songs ever to grace human ears – that of the endangered kokako.

All access and landing permits must be pre-booked well in advance with **DoC** ① *18 Manners St, Wellington T04-3847770, doc.govt.nz, Mon-Fri 0900-1630, Sat-Sun 1000-1500*. Only 50 people can land per day; permits cost $11, child $5 (available on-line).

Paekakariki

Paekakariki is a tiny seaside village, popular with train enthusiasts. But before looking at locos take the 3-km diversion up to the viewpoint on Paekakariki Hill Road. On a clear day there are great views of Kapiti Island and the coast right up to Wanganui. At the village

Bulls

The small agricultural service town of Bulls stands off the junction of SH3 and SH1, midway between Wanganui and Palmerston North. Blink and you'll miss it, but take a closer look and you may be surprised to learn that the township was not named after our four-legged friends, but after James Bull, who was one of the first settlers in 1858. By all accounts he was quite the entrepreneur and created so much of the town's infrastructure that in 1872 the government approved the replacement of the original name for the settlement – Rangitikei – with Bulls. However, our James has a lot to answer for. In the desperate effort to put Bulls on the map, the community has gone to ridiculous lengths to incorporate its name into every one of its amenities. Take a look around and you'll find the i-SITE visitor centre, which is 'Inform- a-Bull', the chemist which is 'Dispense-a-Bull', the fire station 'Extinguish-a-Bull', the police station 'Const-a-Bull' and the church, which is 'Forgive-a-Bull', and so it goes on. However, there are a few major omissions including, as you head out on SH3, a sign saying 'Antiques and Collectibles' – clearly owned by a right misera-bull. Annoyingly, this is very infectious, and for days you will find yourself suffering from this 'Voca-Bull-ary' affliction. Some may find Bulls entertaining, but others may find such behaviour total bullocks.

railway station train buffs will enjoy the **Paekakariki Rail and Heritage Museum** ① *pspt. wellington.net.nz, open Sat and Sun*, where devoted enthusiasts have restored a number of vintage trains, some of which still huff and puff along the tracks. A few kilometres further north is the **Wellington Tramway Museum** ① *Queen Elizabeth Park, T04-292 8361, wellingtontrams.org.nz, $10, child $5, Sat-Sun 1100-1630*, where historical displays look back at one of Wellington's former modes of transport. Several trams are currently in operation in Queen Elizabeth Park and rides are available. The beach at Paekakariki is also worth a look and typical of the area with its piles of driftwood, a deposit from the South Island's West Coast.

Palmerston North

On the banks of the Manawatu River and in the heart of flat, rural Manawatu is the pleasant university and agricultural service town of Palmerston North. Although set away from SH1, Palmy can provide a good base from which to explore the southern half of the North Island and is an important gateway west, through the impressive Manawatu Gorge, to the Wairarapa and Hawkes Bay. Other than Massey University, which is the second largest in the country, the town is perhaps most famous for its rugby museum, a place of almost spiritual significance, where many New Zealand rugby fanatics come on a pilgrimage to pay homage to their All Black heroes.

New Zealand Rugby Museum

① *87 Cuba St, T06-358 6947, rugbymuseum.co.nz. Daily 1000-1700, $12.50, child $5.*
Established in 1969, it was the first of its kind in the country and contains the largest collection of rugby memorabilia including shirts, caps, photographs and programmes. There are also videos and detailed accounts of every All Black game since 1870 available for specialist research. If you have a particular question there is a wealth of fanatics on hand to fill you in on every pass, ruck and maul.

Palmerston North

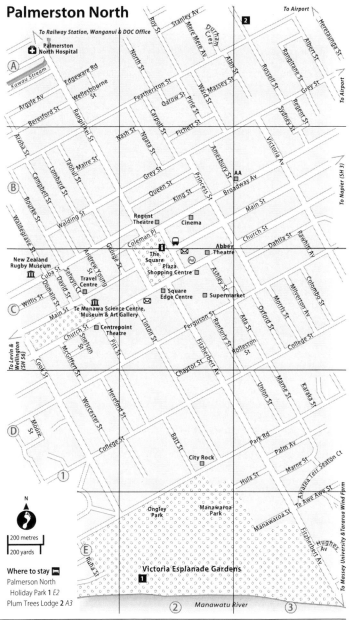

To Airport

2 To Railway Station, Wanganui & DOC Office

Palmerston North Hospital

Kawau Stream

Edgeware Rd
Wellesbourne St
Argyle Av
Beresford St
Aroha St
Campbell St
Lombard St
Bourke St
Walding St
Waldegrave St
New Zealand Rugby Museum
Cuba St
David St
Selwyn St
Andrew Young St
George St
Willis St
Main St
Church St
Pitt St
Cook St
McGregor St
Moore St
Hereford St
Worcester St

Roy St
Stanley Av
Mere Mere Av
Durham Cres
Alan St
North St
Featherston St
Oarow St
Pine St
Carroll St
Ward St
Massey St
Nash St
Ngata St
Fichett St
Grey St
Maire St
Taonui St
Amesbury St
Queen St
King St
Princess St
AA
Broadway Av
Regent Theatre
Cinema
Coleman Pl
The Square
Plaza Shopping Centre
Abbey Theatre
Travel Centre
Te Manawa Science Centre, Museum & Art Gallery
Square Edge Centre
Supermarket
Centrepoint Theatre
Ashley St
Ferguson St
Linton St
Liston St
Main St
Church St
Rangitikei St

To Levin & Wellington (SH 56)

College St
Bart St
City Rock
Park Rd
Palm Av
Marne St
Hula St
Union St
Karaka St
Chaytor St
Fitcherbert Av
Rangfy St
Rotherton St
Ada St
Oxford St
Morris St
College St
Colombo St
Milverton Av
Roxwin Av
Dahlia St
Church St
Main St
Victoria Av
Sydney St
Regent St
Grey St
Rangitane St
Albert St
Russell St
Heretaunga St
To Airport
To Napier (SH 3)

Moore St

Ongley Park
Manawaroa Park
Ruha St
Manawaroa St
Fitcherbert Av
Hughes Av
Te Awe Awe St
Awarea Terr
Seaton Ct
To Massey University & Tararua Wind Farm

1 Victoria Esplanade Gardens

Manawatu River

N

200 metres
200 yards

Where to stay 🛏
Palmerston North
  Holiday Park **1** *E2*
Plum Trees Lodge **2** *A3*

Te Manawa Science Centre, Museum and Art Gallery
ⓘ *396 Main St, T06-355 5000, temanawa.co.nz. Daily 1000-1700, free entry to some galleries*
Te Manawa is a progressive and modern centre that integrates the usual social, cultural and artistic heritage with hands-on science displays. It is split into three main parts the museum, gallery and science centre, all of which are worth visiting. There are some interesting Maori taonga and a few nationally significant artworks by contemporary gurus like Colin McCahon and Ralf Hotere. The gallery often hosts national touring exhibitions.

Te Apiti and Tararua Wind Farms
Well before arriving in Palmy you will no doubt have seen the small forest of white blades that make up the Te Apiti and Tararua Wind Farm on the ranges east of the town. With almost 200 turbines this is one of the largest wind farm sites in the southern hemisphere and a great testimony to clean, renewable energy in New Zealand. It is well worth going to take a closer look and you can do so in the heart of the Te Apiti site via the town of Ashhurst. From Palmerston North, turn off SH3 at Ashhurst and follow the Saddle Road signs. A visitor car park underneath one of the turbines has views of the wind farm and an information display.

If you do not have your own transport you can join a quad bike tour. From Ashhurst you may consider returning to Palmerston North via the **Pohangina Valley Tourist Route**, which takes in a combination of rural scenery, gardens, craft outlets and the town of Feilding. The i-SITE visitor centre can provide details.

Kapiti Coast and Palmerston North listing

For hotel and restaurant price codes and other relevant information, see pages 9-14.

◯ Where to stay

Palmerston North *p112, map p113*
$$ Plum Trees Lodge, 97 Russell St, T06-358 7813, plumtreeslodge.com. Well-appointed, self-contained and within walking distance to the town centre.
$$-$ Palmerston North Holiday Park, 133 Dittmer Dr, T06-358 0349, holidayparks. co.nz/palmerstonnorth. A bit dated but has all the necessary facilities and is located in a peaceful spot next to the river and Esplanade Park.

◯ What to do

Kapiti Coast *p111*
Boat trips
Boat transport to Kapiti Island is available through **Kapiti Marine Charter**, T04-297 2585, T0800-433779, kapitimarinecharter. co.nz and **Kapiti Tours Ltd**, T04-237 7965, T0800 527 484, kapititours.co.nz, from $55, child $30. Boats depart from the Kapiti Boating Club, Paraparaumu Beach. **Kapiti Island Alive**, T06-362 6606, kapitiislandalive. co.nz, offer Maori-themed day trips to the northern end of the island, departing 0900 or 1430 with 1-hr guided walks ($20). Overnight kiwi-spotting trips are also a possibility but book well ahead.

◯ Transport

Palmerston North *p112, map p113*
Palmerston North has air and bus services. Contact **TranzMetro**, T0800-801700, tranzmetro.co.nz. The main i-SITES can assist with bookings.

The Wairarapa

The Wairarapa is one of the least-visited regions in the North Island. Most visitors miss it out in their rush to reach Wellington via SH1, which lies to the west beyond the natural barrier of the Ruahine and Tararua ranges. If that simple fact is not appealing enough, the remote and stunning coastal scenery and relaxed atmosphere will, if you make the effort to visit, confirm that this is a place worth getting to know. The highlights, other than the delights of rural towns like Martinborough, which lie like a string of pearls along SH2, are the ever-increasing number of quality vineyards, a terrific range of country B&Bs and the coastal splendour of Castlepoint and Cape Palliser, the North Island's most southerly point.

Taumatawhakatangihangakoauauotamat eaturipukakapikimaungahoronuku-pokaiwhenuakitanatahu

Try reading that while driving, in fact, try reading it at all. By all accounts this is the longest place name in the world – and you thought it was that train station in Wales. It is Maori (obviously), has 85 letters and roughly translated, it means *'The place where Tamatea, the man with the big knees, who slid, climbed and swallowed mountains (known as land eater) played his flute to his loved one'*.

Well what a boy. For the sake of it, it is worth the trip to see the ludicrously latitudinous sign that points at – won't write it again – but it does involve a bit of a hike and you should kick back and enjoy the back country drive either north or south and take a look (indeed stay) at the charming little coastal enclaves of Herbertville and/or Castlepoint en route. To get to the sign from Waipukurau (north), take the SH52 coast road towards Porangahau. The sign is a few kilometres south of Porangahau on SH52 to Wimbledon. SH52 re-emerges on SH2 at either Eketahuna or Masterton. This will allow you to take in the stunning Castlepoint on the way.

Castlepoint

It is a major diversion to get to this remote coastal settlement (65 km from Masterton) but the trip is well worth it. Castlepoint is considered to be the highlight on the Wairarapa's wild and remote coastline and it certainly deserves the honour. At the eastern end of the main beach a stark rocky headland, from which sprouts the Castlepoint Lighthouse, sweeps south to enclose a large lagoon. The picturesque bay, which is itself a popular spot with surfers and swimmers, is dominated at its southern entrance by the aptly named 162-m Castle Rock, which can be accessed from the southern end of the bay. The lighthouse can be accessed across the sand tombolo, which connects it to the mainland via a boardwalk. Just below the lighthouse there is a cave that can be explored at low tide, but beware – Maori legend has it that it is the hiding place of a huge menacing octopus.

Masterton

The chief commercial centre for the Wairarapa Region, Masterton gives Te Kuiti in the Waikato (the 'sheep-shearing capital of New Zealand') a run for its money in the big woolly event stakes. The Golden Shears is the major date in the local young farmers' calendar and offers moderate fame and fortune to the fastest clipper around. It is held at the beginning of March and lasts about four days.

Alongside the **i-SITE visitor centre** ① *corner Dixon and Bruce Streets, T06-3700900, wairarapanz.com*, is the **Aratoi Wairarapa Museum of Art and History** ① *T06-370 0001, aratoi.co.nz, daily 1000-1630, donation*, which admirably showcases many aspects of the area's social, cultural and natural history, as well as rapidly blossoming into the main focus for local contemporary artists. There's also a good in-house café. Alongside Aratoi is the **Wool Shed** ① *12 Dixon St, T06-378 8008, sheardiscovery.co.nz, daily 1000-1600, $5, child $2*. Developed in two relocated former woolsheds it offers 'a fine round-up' of the shearing and weaving process and showcases the champions of the prized annual Golden Shears contest. Also within walking distance is the much-loved and celebrated **Queen Elizabeth Park**, first planted in 1878.

Pukaha Mount Bruce National Wildlife Centre

① *30 km north of Masterton on SH2 T06-375 8004, mtbruce.org.nz. Daily 0900-1630, $20, children $6.*

This centre is the flagship of DoC's conservation and endangered species breeding programme. Although much of what happens at Mount Bruce takes place behind the scenes (and involves dedicated staff acting as surrogate mothers), the public can see many species otherwise rarely seen. There is something very special about sitting on the veranda of the café, sipping a coffee and overlooking an enclosure with a takahe (a charming prehistoric-looking purple bird, not dissimilar to a large chicken) going happily about its business in the knowledge that there are only 200 or so left in the world. Likewise, taking a stroll through the native bush, to see other enclosures hiding stitchbirds and kokako, all of which you will probably never see again in your lifetime.

There is a nocturnal kiwi house that rates among the best in the country and leaves you in no doubt as to the numerous threats which this national icon faces in the modern world. Other highlights include the eel feed at 1330 and the kaka feed at 1500. The latter should certainly not be missed. Within the main building there are some fine displays, a shop and a café.

Carterton, Waiohine Gorge and Greytown

Located 22 km west of Carterton and at the entrance to the **Tararua Forest Park** the Waiohine Gorge is well worth a visit for the scenery itself, let alone the walks on offer and the heart-stopping **swing bridge**, one of the longest in New Zealand. The road is signposted just south of the town on SH2. Eventually an unsealed road connects you with the riverbank, which gradually rises high above the river gorge. At the road terminus you can embark on a number of walks all of which involve the initial negotiation of the swing bridge that traverses the gorge at a height of about 40 m. If you do nothing else at Waiohine, a few trips back and forth on the bridge is great fun. Although it is perfectly safe, jelly has less wobble.

While in Carterton you may like to visit the **Paua Shell Factory** ① *54 Kent St, T06-379 4222, pauashell.co.nz, daily 0800-1700, free*, one of the few places in the country that converts the stunningly beautiful paua (abalone) shells into jewellery and souvenirs. Further south

Greytown, one is the prettiest of the Wairarapa settlements best known for its antiques, art and craft shops and roadside cafés. It's a great spot to stop for a coffee or lunch.

Martinborough

Martinborough is located towards the coast from SH2, 16 km southeast of Greytown. First settled by nationalistic Briton John Martin in the late 1880s, the village square and the streets running off it form the shape of the Union Jack. With names like Kansas, Texas and Ohio, it is clear that Martin had as much a love of the US as he did his homeland. Described as a unique 'wine village', with over 20 vineyards within walking distance of the square, and blessed with as many charming B&Bs, it is a favourite romantic haunt for Wellingtonians in search of a weekend away. The local **i-SITE visitor centre** ⓘ *18 Kitchener St, T06-306 5010, wairarapanz.com, daily 0900-1600*, can provide all the vineyard detail and a Vintage Village Heritage Walk leaflet that will pinpoint sites of historical interest. The most dominant is the grand and recently restored Martinborough Hotel that is just one of many excellent places to stay. It also has a good restaurant.

The coast road to Cape Palliser

The day-long drive to see the Cape Palliser Lighthouse epitomizes the Wairarapa region and is highly recommended. On the way you can take in the bizarre rock formations of the Putangirua Pinnacles, the charming coastal fishing village of Ngawi and a colony of enchantingly languid fur seals, before the road terminates at the steps of the lighthouse. To get there from Featherston or Martinborough make your way down Lake Ferry Road, towards Lake Ferry. Just before the village turn left for Ngawi. From here the lighthouse is about 40 km.

After about 15 km look out for the **Putangirua Pinnacles** car park. The pinnacle formations are a series of gravel spires and turrets and have reached a new level of popularity after being used as a backdrop in the *Lord of the Rings* film trilogy. They are about an hour's walk down a streambed, so take proper footwear. Don't miss the viewpoint accessed from the main pathway.

From the car park the road continues, hugging the cliffs before opening out across a wide coastal plain, with a beautiful shore of rock and sand, well known for its excellent surfing. The coastal village of **Ngawi** soon comes into view and you will be struck by the collection of old tractors and bulldozers on the beachfront with rigs supporting a raft of fishing boats of all shapes and sizes.

From Ngawi the red and white tower of the lighthouse can soon be seen. On the rocks just before it is a colony of New Zealand fur seals though you will probably smell them before you see them. Like fat, brown barrels they doze the day away amongst the boulders turning scratching and wanton flatulence in to an art form. All they're missing is a TV, a beer and a remote control. Take a closer look, but do not go nearer than 10 m. If you do, their soporific attitude will evaporate in an explosion of rippling blubber as they charge towards the surf.

From the seal colony it is only a short distance to the lighthouse with its steep climb of steps and rewarding views. How many steps? Go on, count! This is the southernmost tip of the North Island. Once you return to Lake Ferry Road it is worth the short diversion to see Lake Ferry itself. The beach, which must endure its fair share of wild weather, is a favourite venue in summer for fishing. The hotel serves good beer and food.

The Wairarapa listings

For hotel and restaurant price codes and other relevant information, see pages 9-14.

● Where to stay

Castlepoint *p115*
Motor parks
$$-$ Castlepoint Holiday Park and Motels, Jetty Rd, T06-372 6705, castlepoint. co.nz. Well off the beaten track in a stunning location. Spacious motor park with adequate amenities right next to the beach. Wide range of accommodation options from tent sites to tourist flats. Modern self-contained motel units are also available in the village.

Greytown *p116*
$$$$-$$$ White Swan Country Hotel, Main St, T06-304 8894, thewhiteswan.co.nz. Offers a choice of 7 rooms. There are also suites and studios in a separate wing to the rear of the hotel. Restaurant and bar.

Martinborough *p117*
$$$$ Peppers Martinborough Hotel, The Square, T06-306 9350, peppers.co.nz.

The historic 1882 Martinborough Hotel adds character and sophistication to this Wairarapa village. The elegant, luxury en suite rooms are individually designed and named after some of the region's first settlers.
$$$ Duckback Cottage, 9 Broadway St, T06-306 9933, duckbackcottage.co.nz. Self-contained cottage with open fire and 3 bedrooms. Within walking distance of all amenities.
$$-$ Martinborough Village Camping, corner of Princess and Dublin streets, T06-306 8946, martinboroughcamping.com. Quality motor park with cabins, powered and tent sites all with shared facilities. Wi-Fi and bike hire for vineyard tours.

● Transport

The Wairarapa *p115*
The Wairarapa is served by regional bus and train services. Contact **TranzMetro**, T0800-801700, tranzmetro.co.nz. The main i-SITES can assist with bookings.

Contents

Footnotes

History of New Zealand

The first footprints

Due to its geographic isolation New Zealand was one of the last 'viable' lands to be settled by humans and therefore has a relatively young human history.

Though much debated and a simplification, Maori trace their ancestry to the homelands of 'Hawaiki' and the great Polynesian navigator Kupe, who is said to have made landfall in Northland, around AD 800. Finding the new land viable for settlement, Kupe named it Aotearoa – The Land of the Long White Cloud. Leaving his crew to colonize, Kupe then returned to Hawaiki to encourage further emigration. A century later the first fleet of waka (canoes) arrived in Aotearoa to settle permanently. It was the crew of these canoes that formed the first iwi (tribes) of a new race of people called the Maori.

The ancestral land called Hawaiki is thought to be Tahiti and the Society Islands, but exactly when and how these early Polynesians arrived and how they lived is in doubt. What is known is that they arrived sporadically In canoes and initially though struggling with the colder climate of New Zealand particularly in the South island, they persevered.

By the time the first European explorers arrived the Maori had developed their own culture, based on the tight-knit family unit and a tribal system not dissimilar to the Celts and Scots. In a desire to protect family, food resources and land the Maori, like the Scots, saw their fair share of brutal inter-tribal conflict. The Maori developed a highly effective community and defence system built within fortified villages or pa and cannibalism was also common. By the 16th century they had developed into a successful, fairly healthy, robust race. This period is known as the Classic Period. But despite the Maori successes in colonization, the subsequent environmental damage was dire and irreversible. A classic dynamic of cause and effect was set in place that would compromise the land forever. The Maori and the animals they brought with them (particularly dogs and rats) proved the nemesis of the unspoiled and isolated biodiversity of the land. Now, with the sails of European ships appearing above the horizon it was the Maori themselves who were facing the threat of annihalation.

European exploration

Although rumoured that the French or Spanish were actually the first Europeans to sight New Zealand, the first documented discovery was made in 1642 by Dutch explorer Abel Tasman. Tasman was sent to confirm or otherwise the existence of the hotly rumoured Great Southern Continent (Terra Australis Incognita) and if discovered, to investigate its viability for trade. Tasman's first encounter with the Maori proved hostile and without setting foot on land he fled to Tonga and Fiji. He christened the new land 'Staten Landt' which was later renamed 'Nieuw Zeeland'. It was Tasman's first and last encounter with the new land, but his visit led to New Zealand being put on the world map.

The next recorded European visit occurred with the arrival of the ubiquitous British explorer Captain Cook on board the Endeavour in 1769. It would be the first of three voyages to New Zealand. Cook's first landing, on 7 October in Poverty Bay (North Island) was eventful to say the least, with what proved to be a classic culture clash with the resident Maori. Ignorance and fear on both sides led to a mutual loss of life, but unlike

Tasman, Cook persevered and after further encounters managed to establish a 'friendly' relationship with the new people he called *tangata Maori* (the 'ordinary people').

European settlement and the clash of cultures

After news spread of the Cook voyages it did not take long for European sealers and whalers to reach New Zealand and rape the rich marine resources. By the 1820s the New Zealand fur seal and numerous species of whale had been brought to the verge of extinction. As the industries subsequently declined they were quickly joined or replaced by timber and flax traders. Others including adventurers, ex-convicts from Australia and some very determined (and some would say, much needed) missionaries joined the steady influx. Samuel Marsden gave the first Anglican sermon in the Bay of Islands on Christmas Day, 1814.

Inevitably, perhaps, an uneasy and fractious integration occurred between the Maori and the new settlers (or Pakeha as they were called) and, in tune with the familiar stories of colonized peoples the world over, the consequences for the native people were disastrous. Western diseases quickly ravaged over 25% of the Maori population and the trade of food, land or even preserved heads for the vastly more powerful and deadly European weapons resulted in the Maori Musket Wars 1820-1835. It proved a swift and almost genocidal era of inter-tribal warfare.

With such a melting pot of divergent cultures, greed and religion simmering on a fire of lawlessness and stateless disorganization, New Zealand was initially an awful place to be. Crime and corruption was rife. The Maori were conned into ridiculously unfavourable land-for-weapons deals and, along with the spread of Christianity and disease, their culture and tribal way of life was gradually being undermined. Such were the realities of early settlement that Kororareka (now known as Russell) in the Bay of Islands, which was the largest European settlement in the 1830s, earned itself the name and reputation as the 'Hellhole of the Pacific'. Amidst all the chaos the settlers began to appeal to their governments for protection.

The Treaty of Waitangi

By 1838 there were about 2000 British subjects in New Zealand and by this time the country was under the nominal jurisdiction of New South Wales in Australia. In 1833 James Busby was sent to Waitangi in the Bay of Islands as the official 'British Resident'. He was given the responsibility of law and order, but without the means to enforce it. Chaos reigned and finally, exacerbated by a rumour that the French were threatening to pre-empt any British attempt to claim sovereignty of New Zealand, Britain appointed Captain William Hobson as Lieutenant Governor to replace Busby. His remit was to effect the transfer of sovereignty over the land from the Maori chiefs to the British Crown. With the help of Busby who was now familiar with the ways and desires of the Maori, Hobson created what was to become the most important and controversial document in New Zealand history, the Treaty of Waitangi.

In the hastily compiled document there were three main provisions. The first was the complete cession of sovereignty by the Maori to the Queen of England. The second was the promise of full rights and possession of Maori lands and resources (but with the right to sell, of course). The third, and perhaps the greatest, attraction, given the chaotic environment, was the full rights and protection of Maori as British citizens. After two days of discussions, a few amendments and amidst much pomp and ceremony, over 40 Maori chiefs eventually signed the Treaty on 5 February 1840. With these first few signatures from the predominantly Northland tribes, Hobson went on a tour of the country to secure others.

To this day the Treaty of Waitangi remains a very contentious document. From its very inception it was inevitably going to be a fragile bridge between two very different cultures. Given the many differences in communication, translation and meaning, at best it was spurious or vague but worse still could, as a result, be easily manipulated in both actual meaning and subsequent enactment.

By the September of 1840 Hobson had gathered over 500 signatures, all in the North Island. Feeling this was enough to claim sovereignty over New Zealand he did so, and declaring the right of discovery over the South Island, made New Zealand a Crown Colony, independent of New South Wales and Australia. But the refusal and subsequent omission of several key (and powerful) Maori chiefs paved the way for regional disharmony and eventually war.

Maori (Land) Wars

In 1840 Hobson established Kororareka as the first capital of New Zealand, but given its reputation and history, he moved the seat of government to Auckland. With the increased influx of settlers, all greedy for land and resources, human nature very quickly superseded the legal niceties and undermined the fragile bridge of the new bicultural colony. In a frenzy of very dubious land deals between Maori and Pakeha (white settlers), as well as misunderstandings in methods of land use and ownership, resentment between the two was rife. This, plus the heavy taxes that were being demanded by the new and financially strapped government, strained the bridge to breaking point. The Maori were beginning to feel disenfranchised and began to rebel against British authority.

Legendary and belligerent chiefs like Hone Heke and Te Kooti (who for a time became the most wanted man in the land) put up a determined and courageous fight. But with far superior weaponry and organization the British quickly subdued the rebels. In return for their disobedience, and despite the treaty, they confiscated huge tracts of land. This land was then sold to new or already established settlers. By 1900 over 90% of the land was outside Maori ownership or control. They were a defeated people and, with little or no power and with continued integration, their culture was rapidly crumbling.

Natural resources, consolidation and social reform

Although development suffered as a result of the conflicts, timber, agriculture and gold came to the rescue. With the first discoveries made in the 1850s much of the economic focus shifted to the South Island and the seat of a new central (as opposed to provincial) government was moved to Wellington, which became the capital in 1876. The gold boom saw the Pakeha population grow dramatically and although it lasted only a decade, the infrastructures that it set in place paved the way for agricultural, timber and coal industries to quickly take over. In the agriculture sector alone, especially through sheep and dairy cattle, New Zealand was becoming an internationally significant export nation and prosperity continued. Towards the end of the 19th century the country also went through a dramatic and sweeping phase of social reforms. Well ahead most other Western nations, women secured the vote and pioneering legislation was enacted, introducing old-age pensions, minimum wage structures and arbitration courts.

But again, while the Pakeha prospered the Maori continued to suffer. Despite the Native Lands Act of 1865 that was established to investigate Maori land ownership and distribute land titles, by 1900 the Maori population had decreased to less than 50,000 and with the integration of Maori and Pakeha, pure Maori were becoming even more of a minority.

Prosperity and the world wars

By 1907 New Zealand progressed to the title of 'Dominion' of Britain rather than merely a 'colony' and by the 1920s was in control of most of its own affairs. By virtue of its close links with Britain, New Zealand and the newly formed (trans-Tasman) Australia and New Zealand Army Corps (ANZACs) became heavily embroiled in the Boer War of 1899-1902 and again in the First World War, at Gallipoli and the Western Front. Although noted for their steadfast loyalty, courage and bravery, the ANZACs suffered huge losses. Over 17,000 never returned with one in every three men aged between 20 and 40 being killed or wounded. Their First World War casualties remain the greatest of any combat nation.

After the First World War New Zealand joined the Western world in the Great Depression of the 1920s, but it recovered steadily and independently progressed in an increasing atmosphere of optimism. Again from a solid base of agricultural production it prospered and immigration, particularly from Britain, grew steadily. The population had now passed one million and it was enjoying one of the highest standards of living in the world.

Progress ceased temporarily with the outbreak of the Second World War and once again, the loyal ANZACs answered the call. With the spread of the conflict across the Pacific, it proved a nervous time for the nation, but with the dropping of the atomic bomb in Japan the threat ceased and the war was over.

New Zealand today

Post 1945

In 1947 New Zealand was declared an independent nation but maintained close defence and trade links with the Great Britain, the USA and Australia. In 1945 it became one of the original member states of the United Nations (UN) and later joined the ANZUS Defence Pact with the USA and Australia. Domestically, the country again prospered but the nagging problems of race relations, land and resource disputes between Maori and Pakeha still had to be addressed.

In 1975 significant progress was made with the formation of the Waitangi Tribunal, which was established to legally and officially hear Maori claims against the Crown. This method of addressing the problems continues to this day, but as ever, the misinterpretations of the treaty and its translation remain a major stumbling block.

New Zealand joined most of the developed world in the economic slump of the 1970s and 80s. In response to the economic decline, the government deregulated the country's economy, paving the way for free trade and New Zealand, like Australia, was beginning to see itself playing a far more significant role in the Asian markets as opposed to the traditional European ones.

One of the most important landmark decisions made on foreign policy in the 1980s was New Zealand's staunch anti-nuclear stand. In 1984 it refused entry to any foreign nuclear-powered ships in its coastal waters. This soured its relationship with the US who reacted by suspending defence obligations to New Zealand made under the ANZUS pact in the 1950s. This anti-nuclear stance is still maintained with considerable pride and is one that was only strengthened when the French Secret Service bombed the Greenpeace vessel *Rainbow Warrior* in 1985, causing national and international outrage. Relations with France were further soured in 1995 with the rather arrogant and insensitive testing of nuclear weapons in French Polynesia.

Throughout the 1990s the National Party continued successfully to nurture the free market economic policies first initiated by Labour. In 1999 the Labour Party were re-elected under the leadership of Helen Clarke. Her success as Prime Minister was to prove unprecedented, remaining in power until 2008 when Labour were ousted from government by the National Party under the leadership of new PM John Key.

The new millennium

Given its size and isolation New Zealand enjoyed considerable yet brief worldwide attention when on 1 January 2000 it was the first country to see the dawn of the new millennium. However, less appreciative attention was to follow after the infamous terrorist attacks of 11 September 2001 and the subsequent US-led military interventions in Afghanistan and Iraq. Unlike the Howard government of Australia, the New Zealand government led by Helen Clarke did not to align itself with that US policy and in a way repeated the fracas over the anti-nuclear stance of the 1980s. Most kiwis were very proud of Helen Clark's intelligent and (some say) truly democratic leadership at the time, despite the ramifications in current world affairs. The majority did not want to join the campaign in Iraq and its government rightfully and steadfastly exercised that voice. Kiwis are proud of their country and are more concerned about community and the environment than misguided patriotism, power and politics.

So returning to the shadows (bar the substantial hype surrounding the filming of Lord of the Rings) New Zealand remains a 'low-key' nation largely left to its own devices, blessed by an outstanding natural environment, healthy independence and the huge asset of a low and cosmopolitan population. It is not alone in its current economic struggles of course and a poor exchange rate and the ups and downs of free trade agreements may continue to cause problems as it did before the global financial meltdown.

Its biggest social challenge is the continued and difficult journey down the road of biculturalism as well perhaps as some sensible long-term decisions pertaining to future levels of immigration and eco-tourism. It also has its abiding and mutually respectful yet sometimes fractious relationship with Australia to deal with. But perhaps New Zealand's greatest challenge lies in the conservation and protection of its environment, for which it is most famous and much loved. Indeed, with a world facing the specter of rapid and human induced climate change perhaps it can – like Sweden – set an example for the rest of the world to follow. Dubbed the 'Clean Green Land' it certainly has a reputation to fulfill and an innate respect for environment is certainly there, but it remains to be seen whether its government and people can truly embrace the reality that its relatively healthy ecological condition is in fact probably due to its lack of population, as opposed to the common and traditional human attitudes that have proved to be so ruinous elsewhere.

Index

Titles available in the Footprint *Focus* range

For the latest books, e-books and a wealth of travel information, visit us at: www.footprinttravelguides.com.

footprinttravelguides.com

Join us on facebook for the latest travel news, product releases, offers and amazing competitions: www.facebook.com/footprintbooks.